BORN THIS WAY
LADY GAGA

ISBN 978-1-4584-1225-6

HAL•LEONARD®
CORPORATION

7777 W. BLUEMOUND RD. P.O. BOX 13819 MILWAUKEE, WI 53213

Visit Hal Leonard Online at
www.halleonard.com

MARRY THE NIGHT

Words and Music by STEFANI GERMANOTTA
and FERNANDO GARIBAY

Driving Dance Pop

I'm gon-na mar-ry the night, I won't give up on my life.

I'm a war-ri-or queen, live pas-sion-ate-ly to-night.

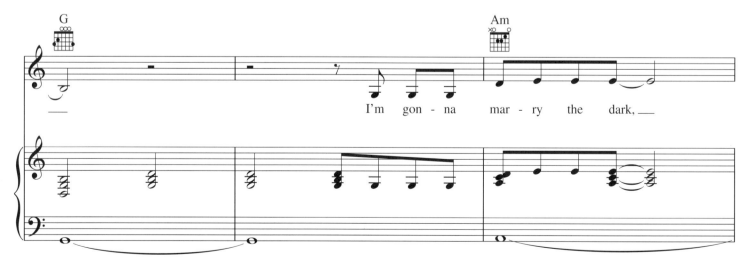

I'm gon-na mar-ry the dark, ___

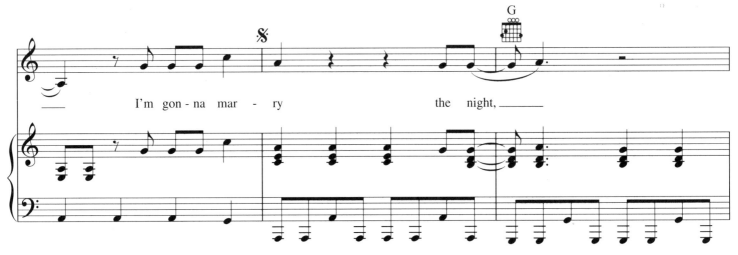

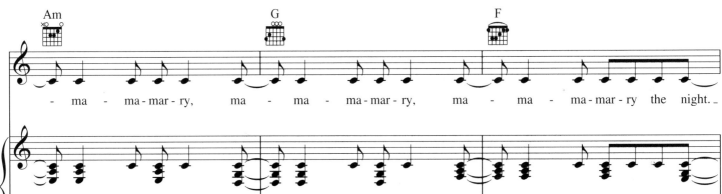

ner. Then I'll go down to the bar, but I won't

cry an-y-more. I'll hold my whis-key up high, kiss the

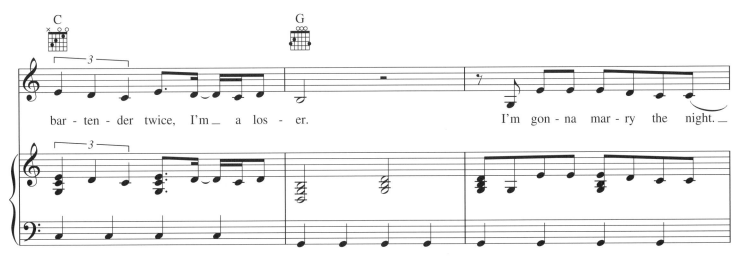

bar-ten-der twice, I'm_ a los-er. I'm gon-na mar-ry the night._

D.S. al Coda

I'm gon-na mar-ry the night. __ I'm gon-na mar -

Noth-ing's _ too cool to take me _ from you.

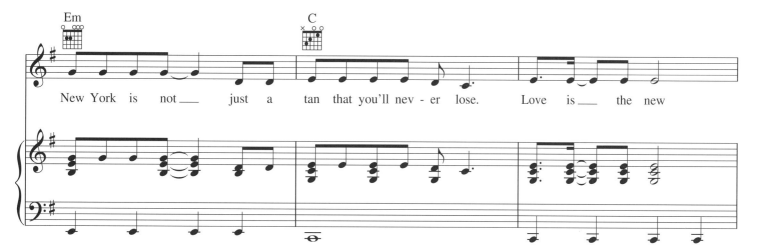

New York is not _ just a tan that you'll nev-er lose. Love is _ the new

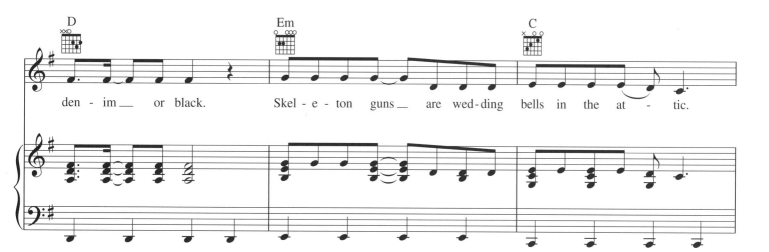

den-im _ or black. Skel-e-ton guns _ are wed-ding bells in the at-tic.

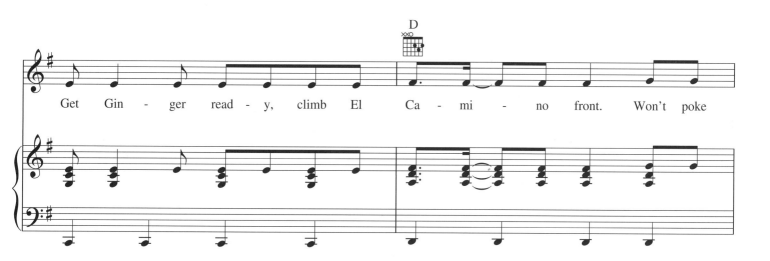

Get Gin-ger read-y, climb El Ca-mi-no front. Won't poke

holes in the ___ seats ___ with my heels 'cause that's where we make ___ love. ___

Come on and run. ___

Turn the car on and run. ___

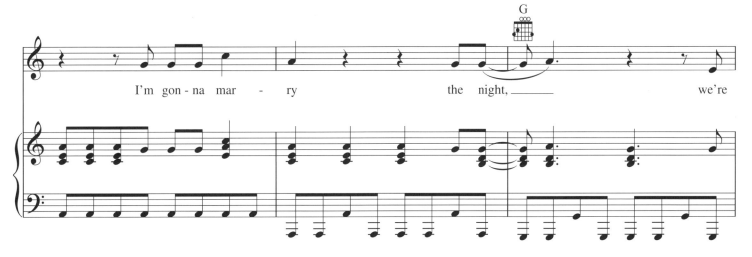

I'm gon-na mar - ry the night, _____ we're

gon - na burn a hole in the road. _____ I'm gon - na mar -

ry the night, _____ leave

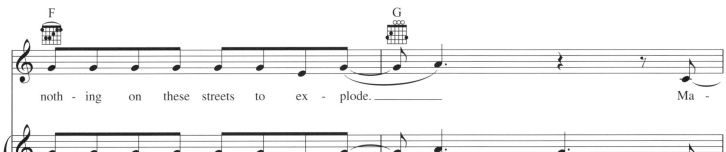

noth - ing on these streets to ex - plode. _____ Ma -

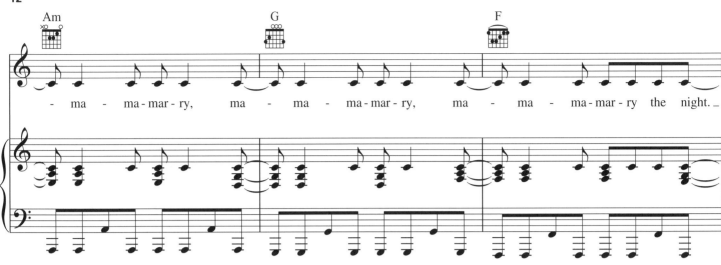

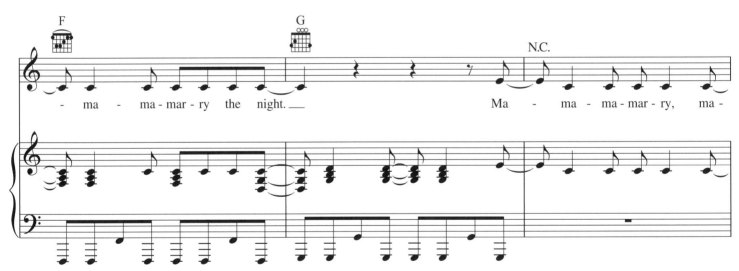

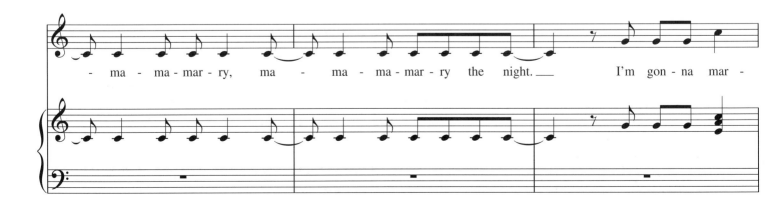

ry.   Mar - ry.

I'm gon - na mar - ry.   Mar -

ry.   Come on.   Come on.   The night,   the night,

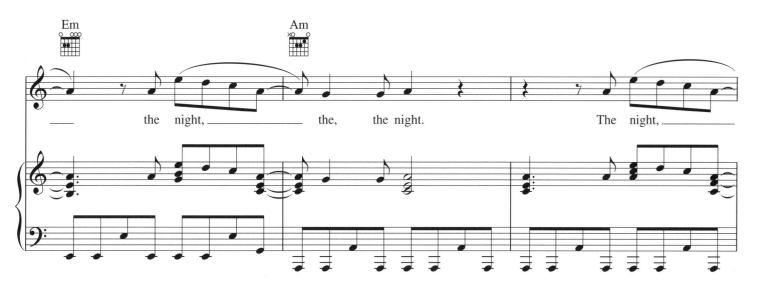

the night,   the,   the night.   The night,

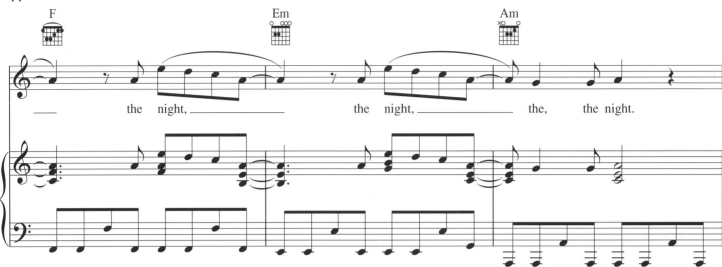

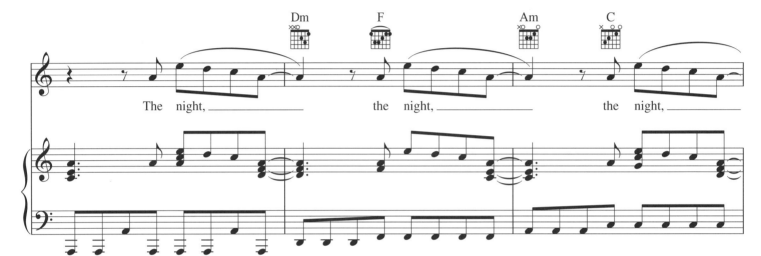

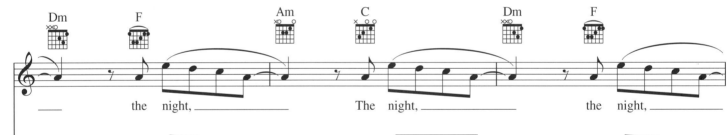

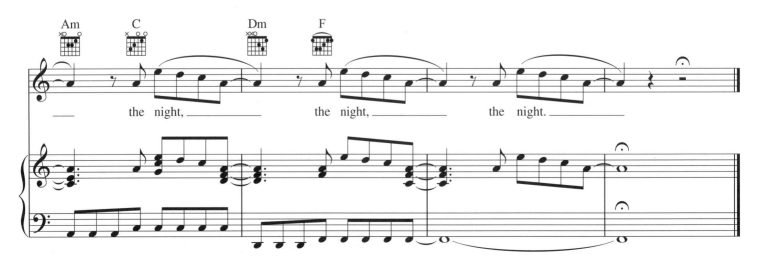

BORN THIS WAY

Words and Music by STEFANI GERMANOTTA,
JEPPE LAURSEN, PAUL BLAIR
and FERNANDO GARIBAY

Energetic Pop

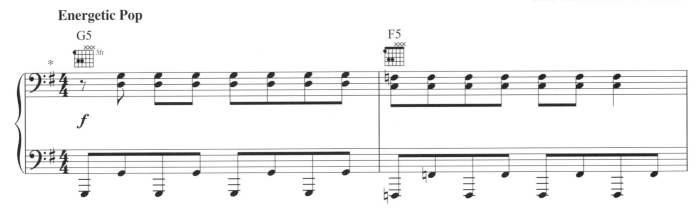

My ma - ma told me when I _____ was young, _____
Give your - self pru - dence and love your friends; _____

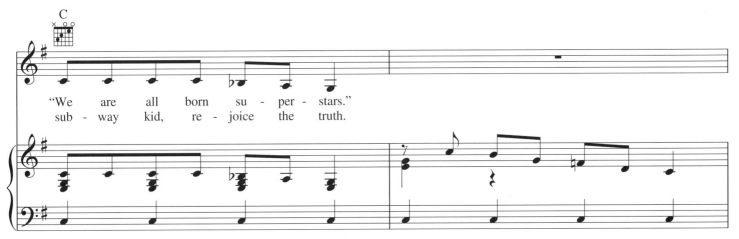

"We are all born su - per - stars."
sub - way kid, re - joice the truth.

* *Recorded a half step lower.*

G

She rolled my hair and put my lip - stick __ on __
In the re - li - gion of the in - se - cure __ I must

C

in the glass of her bou - doir.
be my - self, re - spect my youth.

G   **F**

"There's noth - in' wrong with lov - in' who you are," __ she said,
A dif - f'rent lov - er __ is not a sin, __ be - lieve

C   **G**

"'cause He made you per - fect, babe.
cap - i - tal H - I - M.

So hold your head up, girl, and
I love my life, I love this

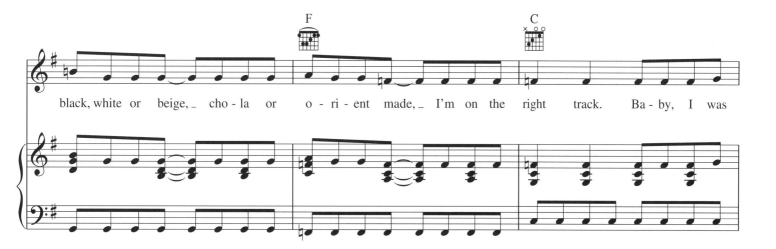

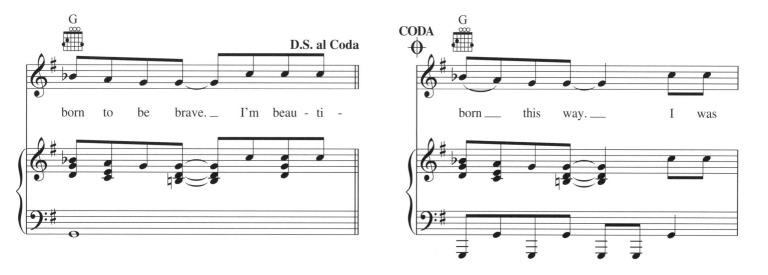

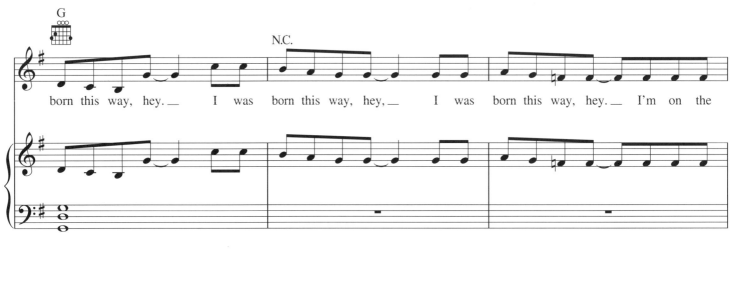

born this way, hey. __ I was born this way, hey, __ I was born this way, hey. __ I'm on the

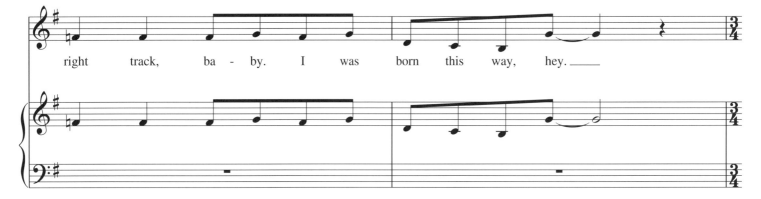

right track, ba - by. I was born this way, hey. ____

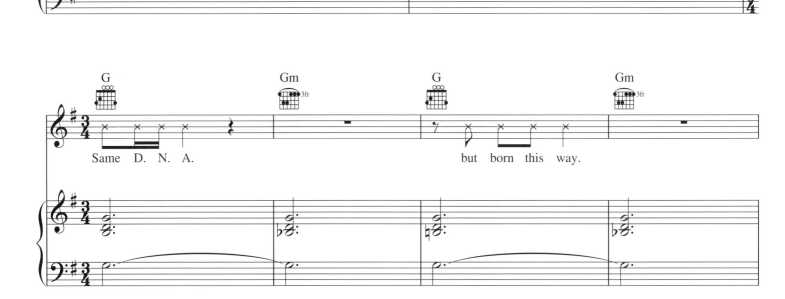

Same D. N. A.   but born this way.

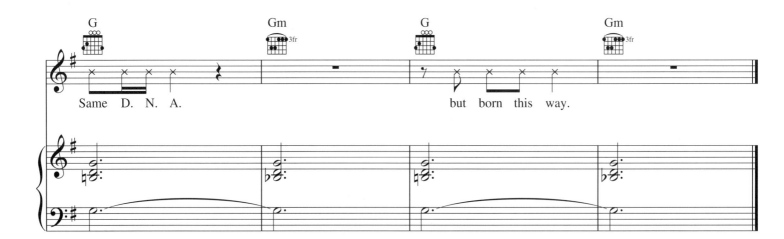

Same D. N. A.   but born this way.

GOVERNMENT HOOKER

Words and Music by STEFANI GERMANOTTA,
PAUL BLAIR, CLINTON SPARKS, FERNANDO GARIBAY
and WILLIAM GRIGAHCINE

Driving Pop

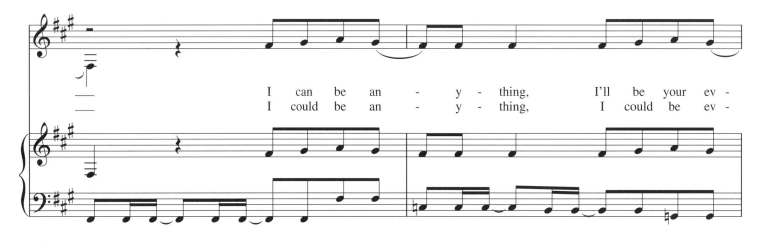

I can be an - y - thing, I'll be your ev -
I could be an - y - thing, I could be ev -

- 'ry - thing. Just touch me, ba - by. (I don't want to be sad.) _
- 'ry - thing. I could be Mom. _ (Un - less you want to be

Dad.) As long as I'm _ your hook - er. (Back

up and turn a - round.) _ As long as I'm _ your hook - er. _

(Hands on the ground.)__ As long as I'm__ your hook - er. (Back

up and turn a - round.)__ As long as I'm__ your hook - er._____

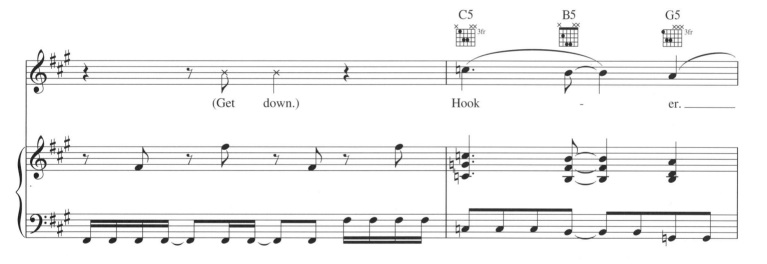

(Get down.) Hook - er._____

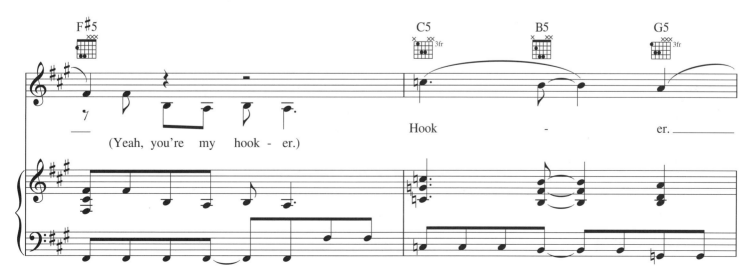

(Yeah, you're my hook - er.) Hook - er._____

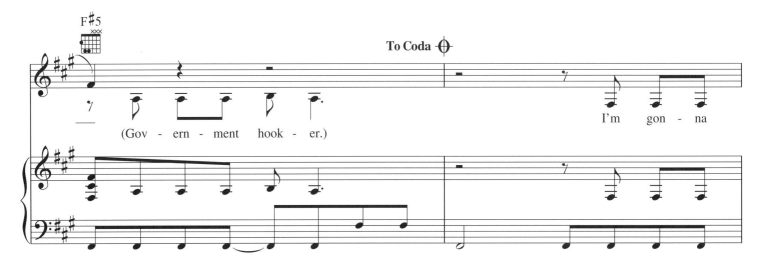

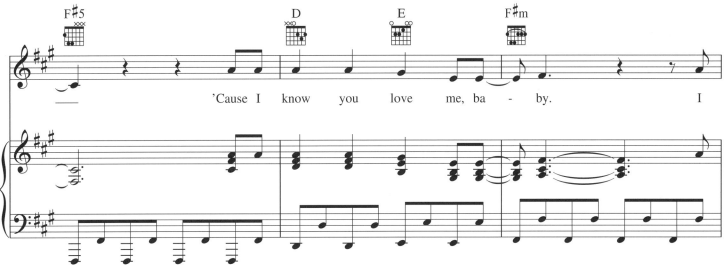

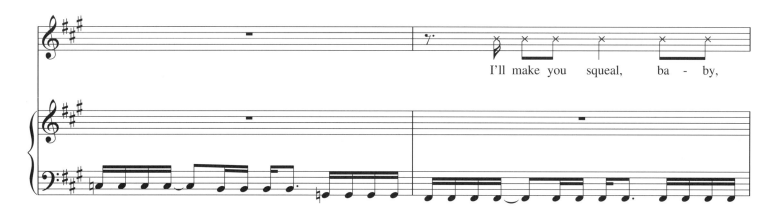

I'll make you squeal, ba - by,

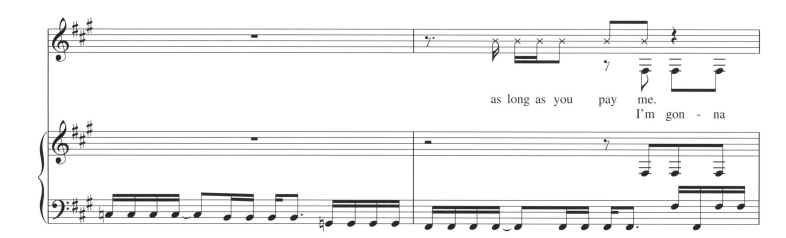

as long as you pay me.
I'm gon - na

drink my tears to - night, ___ I'm gon - na drink my tears and cry. ___

'Cause I know you love me, ba - by. I

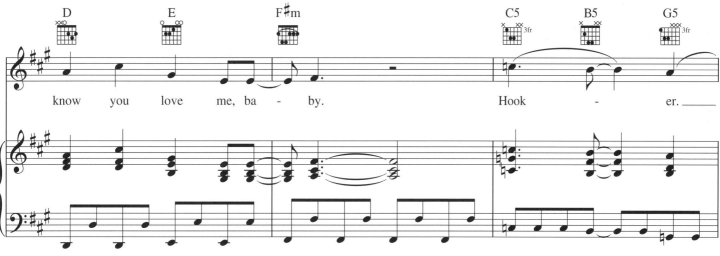

know you love me, ba - by. Hook - er.

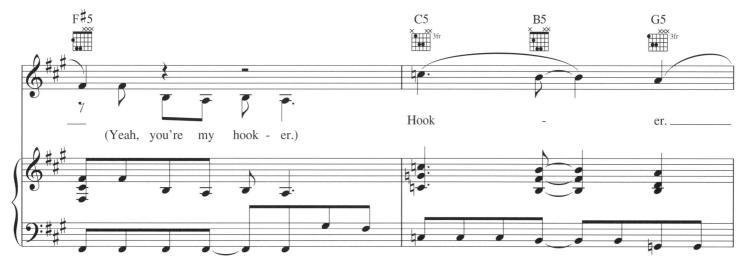

(Yeah, you're my hook - er.) Hook - er.

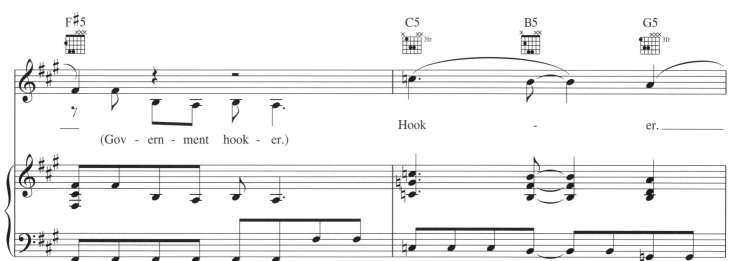

(Gov - ern - ment hook - er.) Hook - er.

(Yeah, you're my hook - er.) Hook - er.

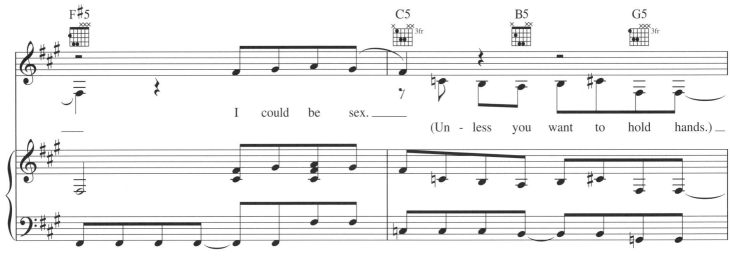

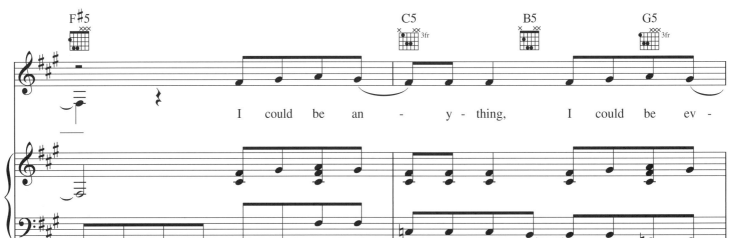

JUDAS

Words and Music by STEFANI GERMANOTTA
and NADIR KHAYAT

Ju - das, Ju - da-ah - ah.   Ju - das, Ju - da-ah - ah.   Ju - das, Ju - da-ah - ah.

Ju - das,   Ga - ga. _____ When he calls to me, I am read -
Ju - das,   Ga - ga. _____ I could - n't love a man so pu - re -

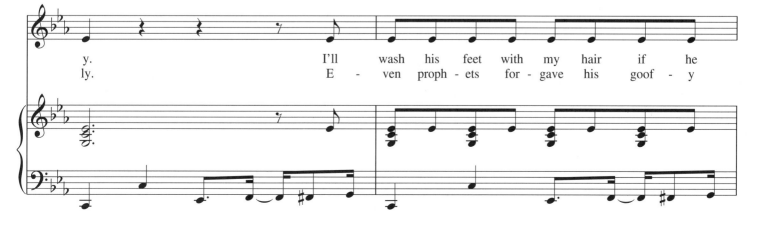

y.   I'll wash his feet with my hair if he
ly.   E - ven proph - ets for - gave his goof - y

needs.
For - give him when his tongue lies through his
way.
I've learned love is like a brick, you

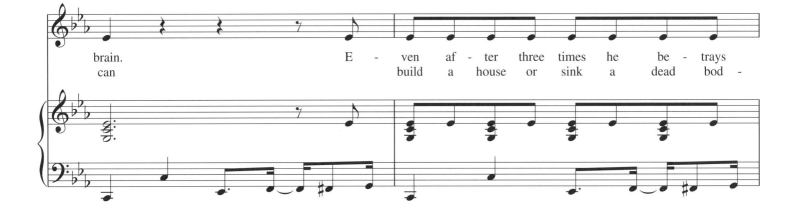

brain.
E - ven af - ter three times he be - trays
can
build a house or sink a dead bod -

Ab   Ab/C   Ab

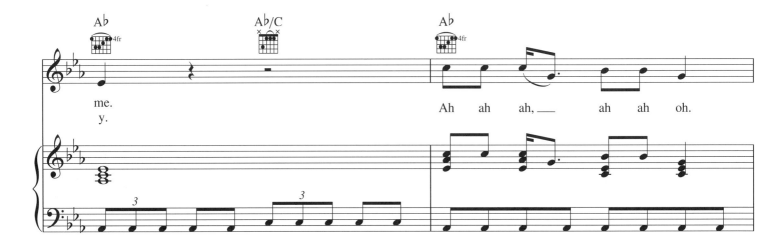

me.
y.
Ah ah ah, __ ah ah oh.

Fm   Cm

Ah ah ah, __ ah ah oh. I'll bring him down, __ bring him

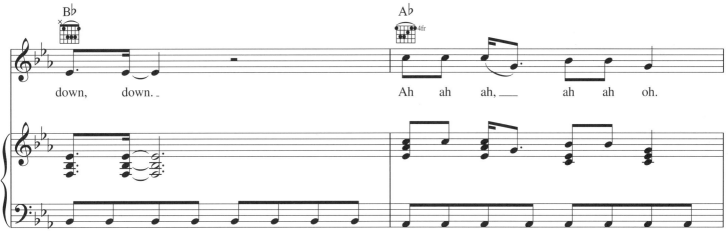

down, down. ___ Ah ah ah, ___ ah ah oh.

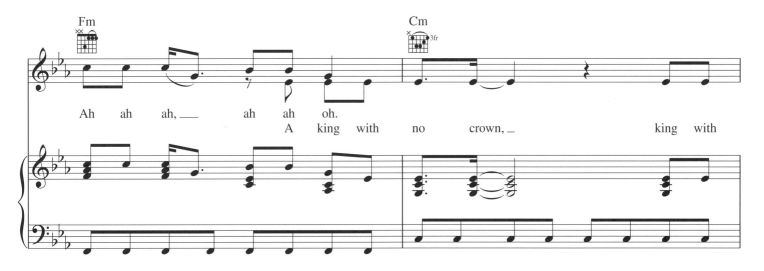

Ah ah ah, ___ ah ah oh. A king with no crown, ___ king with

no crown. ___ I'm just a ho-ly fool, ___ oh, ba-

-by, it's so cruel, ___ but I'm still in love with Ju-das, ba-by. I'm

just a ho-ly fool, _ oh, ba - by, it's so cruel, _ but I'm still in love with Ju - das, ba-

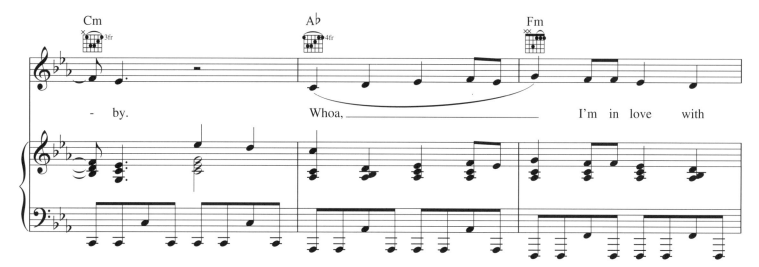

- by.   Whoa, _____   I'm in love   with

Ju - das, _____   Ju - das. _____   Whoa, _____

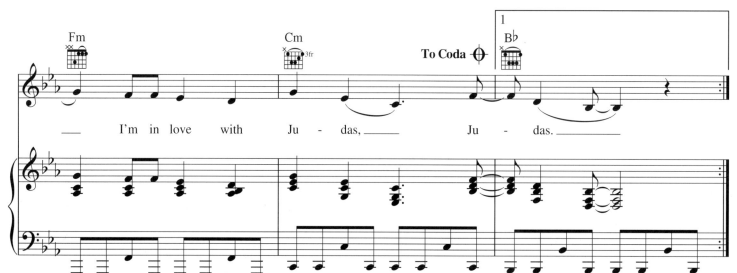

____ I'm in love with Ju - das, _____   Ju - das. _____

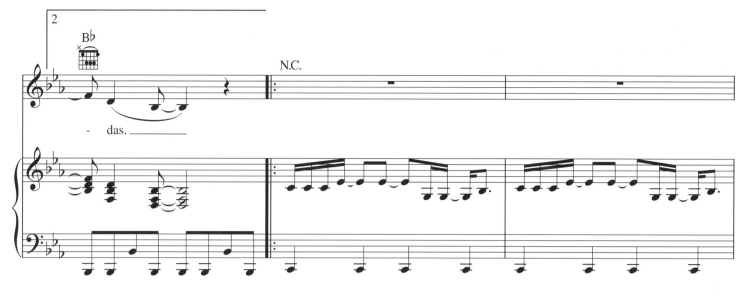

das.

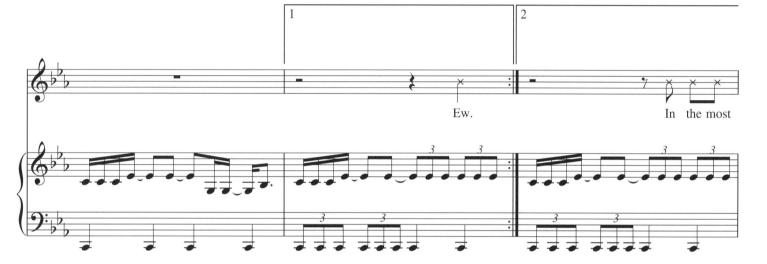

Ew. In the most

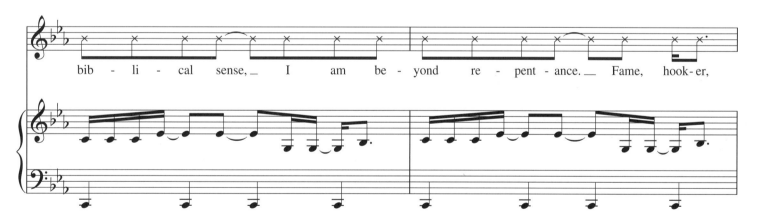

bib - li - cal sense,__ I am be - yond re - pent - ance.__ Fame, hook - er,

pros - ti - tute,__ wench__ vom - its her mind. But in the

38

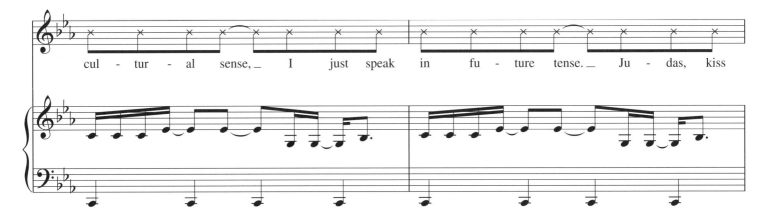

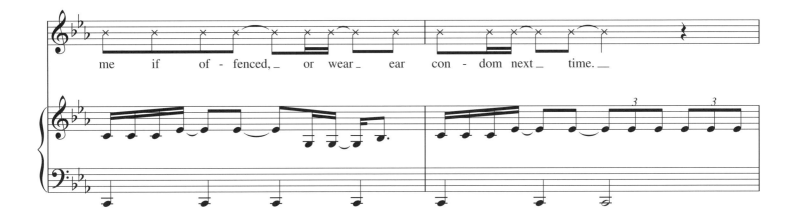

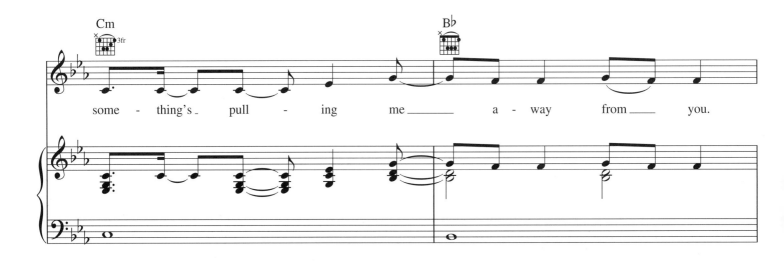

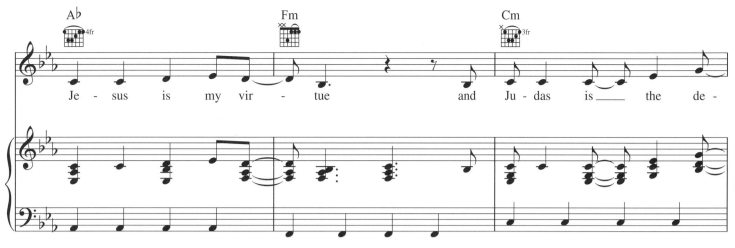

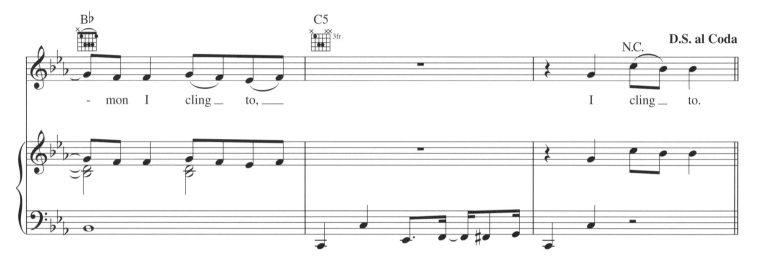

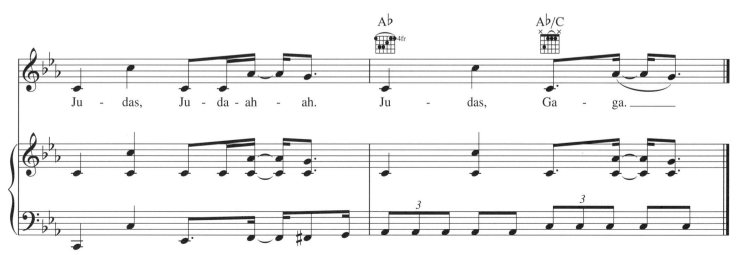

AMERICANO

Words and Music by STEFANI GERMANOTTA,
PAUL BLAIR, FERNANDO GARIBAY
and BRIAN LEE

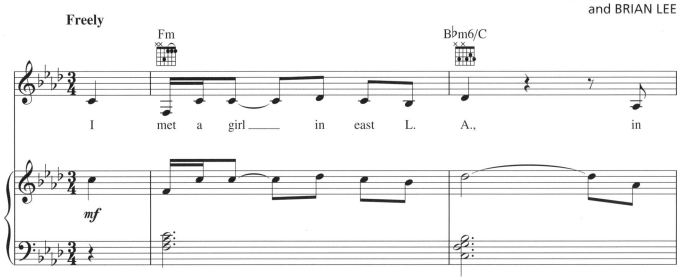

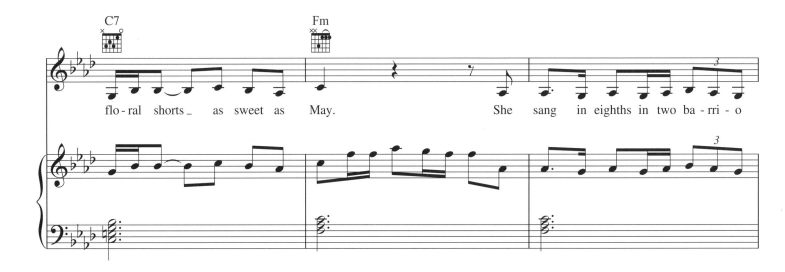

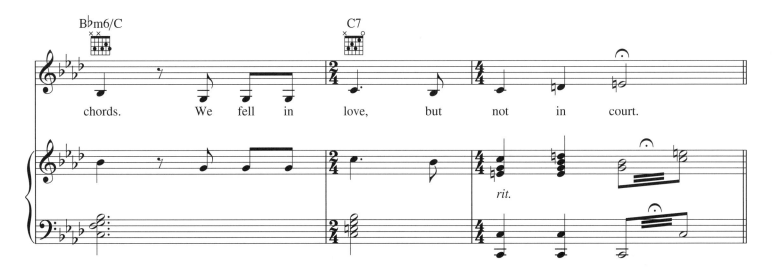

Dance Pop, with a Latin flavor

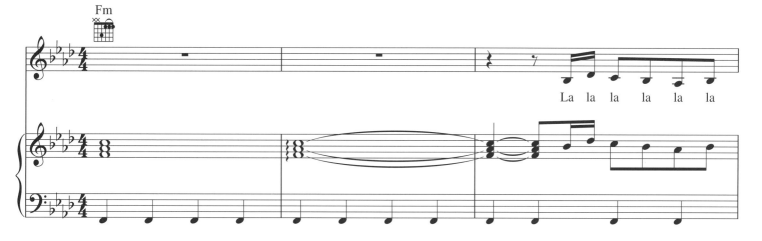

La la la la la la

la. La la la la la la la. La la la la la la la. La la la la la la

la. La la la la la la la. La la la la la la la.

I don't... I don't... Ah,

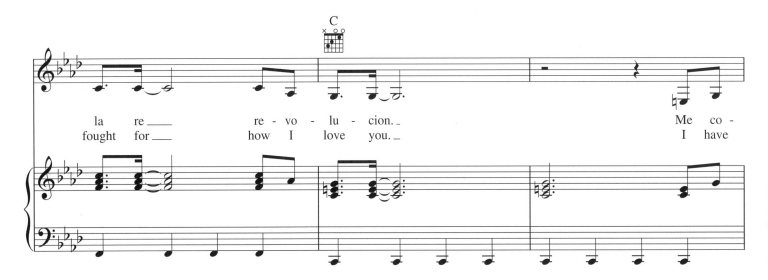

ra - zón ___ me due - le por _____ mi gen - e - ra - ción. _____
cried for, _ I will die for _____ how _ I ____ care. _____

If you love me, we can mar - ry on the
In the moun - tains las cam - pa - nas ___ Es - tán so -

West coast.
nan - do. On a Wednes - day, ___ en el ve -
To - dos los chi - cos, ___ Y los

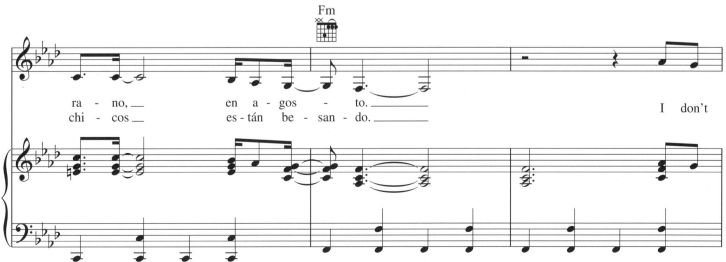

ra - no, ___ en a - gos - to. _____
chi - cos __ es - tán be - san - do. _____ I don't

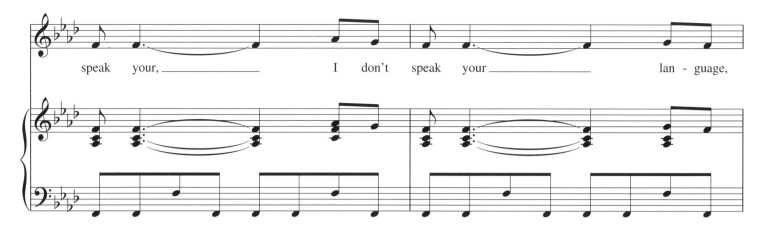

speak your, _____ I don't speak your _____ lan - guage,

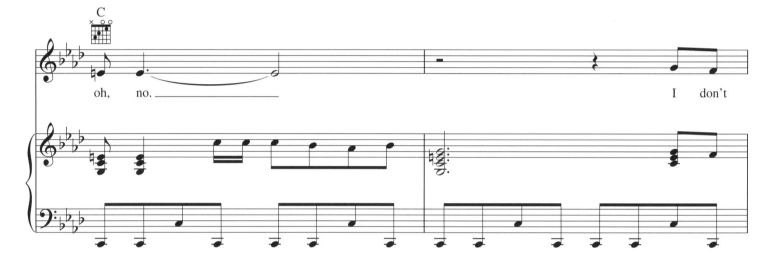

C

oh, no. _____ I don't

C7

speak your, _____ I $\left\{\begin{array}{c}\text{don't}\\\text{won't}\end{array}\right\}$ speak your _____ Je - sus

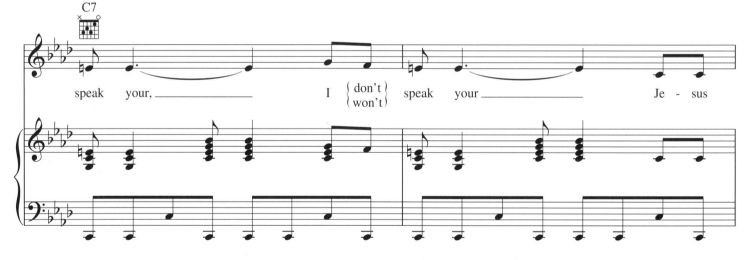

Fm

Chris - to. _____

1

Ah. _____

2

I don't

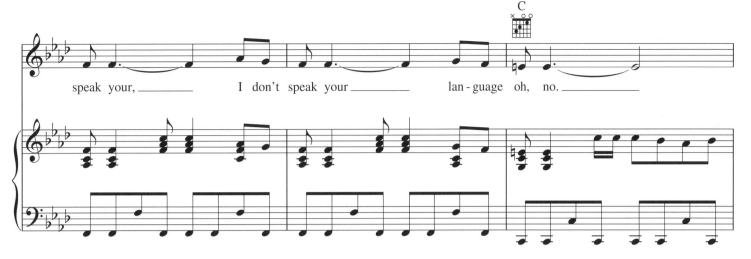

speak your, _____ I don't speak your _____ lan - guage oh, no. _____

I don't speak your, _____ I don't speak your _____ Je - sus

Chris - to. _____ Ah, _____ A - mer - i -

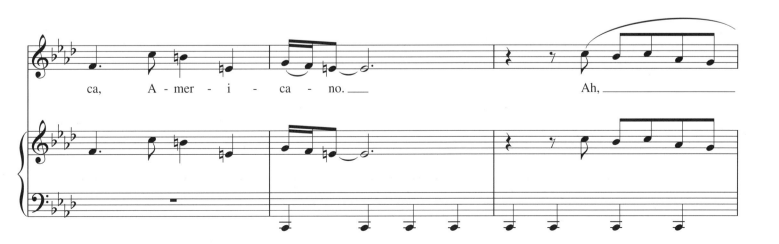

ca, A - mer - i - ca - no. _____ Ah, _____

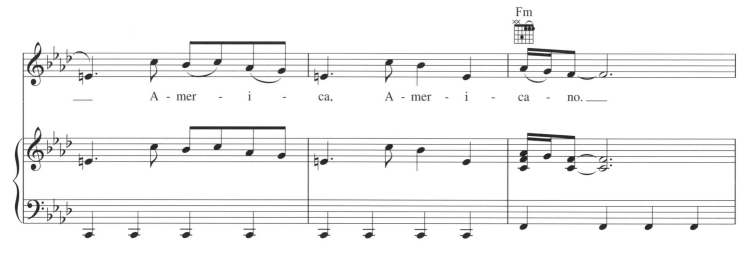

America, Americano.

Ah, America, Ameri-

ca-no. Ah, Ameri-

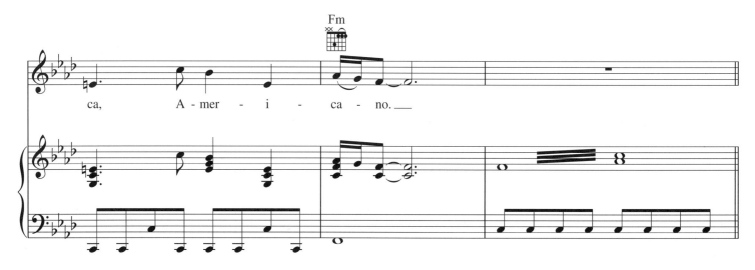

ca, America-no.

Don't you try to catch me, don't ___ you try to catch me, catch
get me,

no, no, ___ no, ___ no. I'm liv-ing on the edge of, liv-
Don't you try to catch me,

- ing on the edge of the law, ___ law, ___ law, law.

1

2

law.

HAIR

Words and Music by STEFANI GERMANOTTA
and NADIR KHAYAT

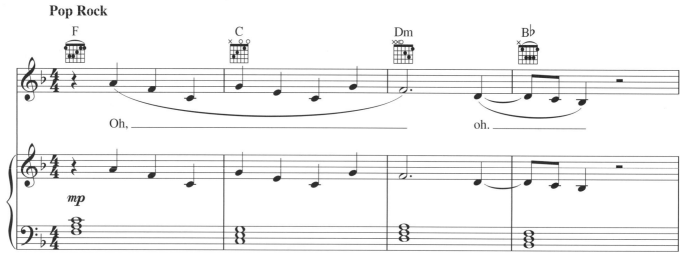

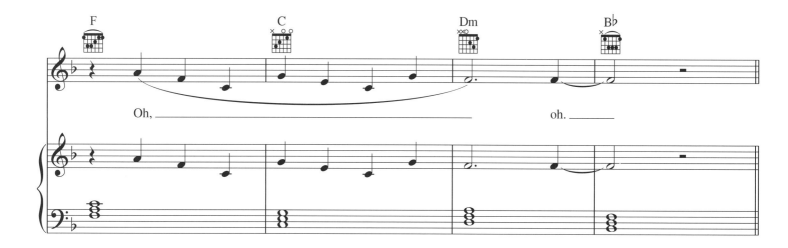

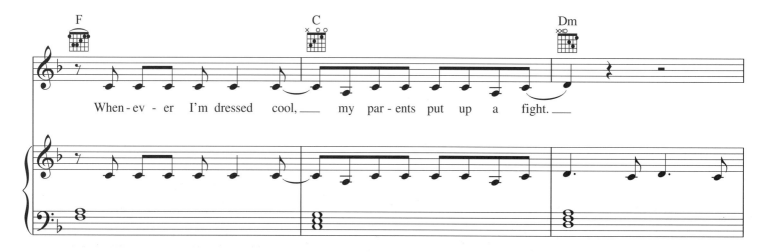

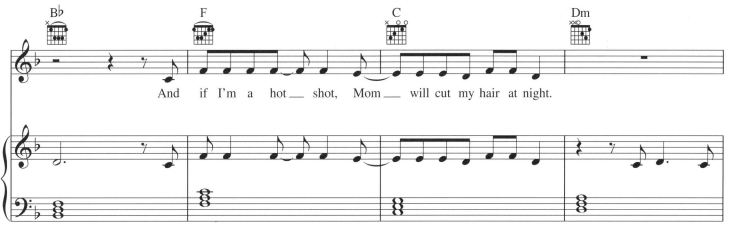

And if I'm a hot shot, Mom will cut my hair at night.

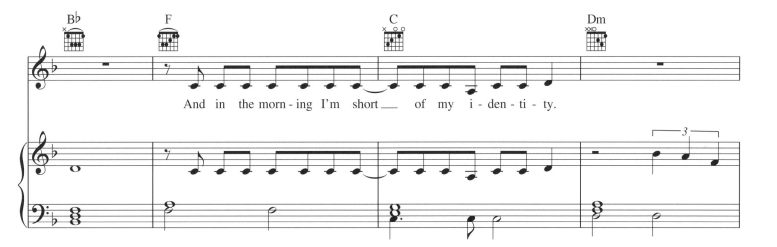

And in the morn-ing I'm short of my i-den-ti-ty.

I scream, "Mom and Dad, why can't I be who I want to be, to be?"

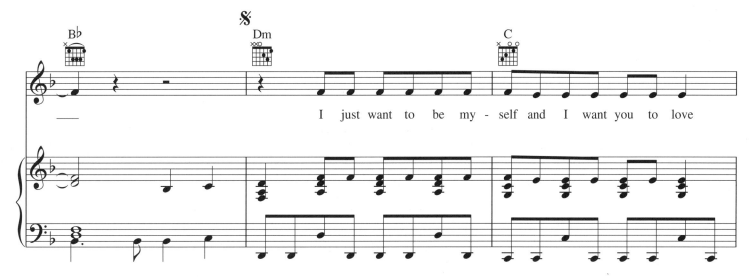

I just want to be my-self and I want you to love

me for who I am. _____ I just want to be my-

self and I want you to know I am my hair. I've had e - nough, __

__ this is my prayer __ that I'll die liv - ing just as free as my hair.

__ I've had e - nough, __ this is my prayer __ that I'll die

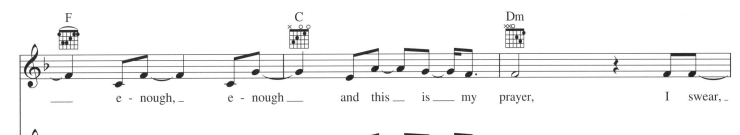

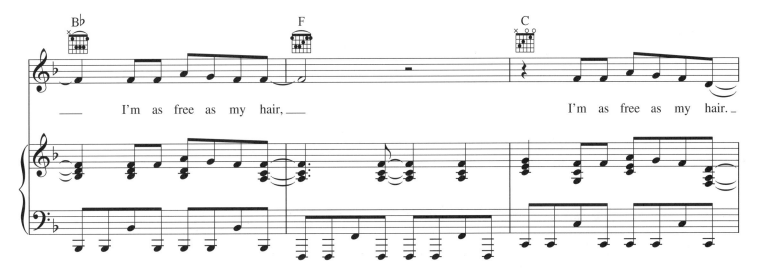

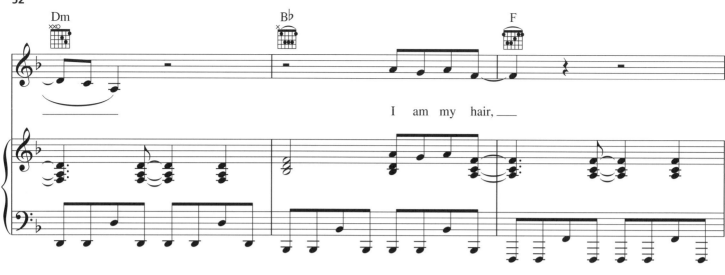

I am my hair, ___

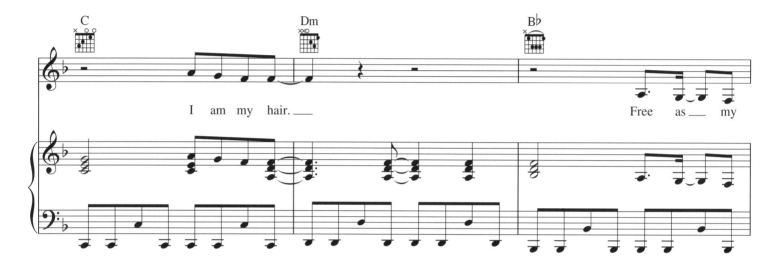

I am my hair. ___   Free as ___ my

hair.

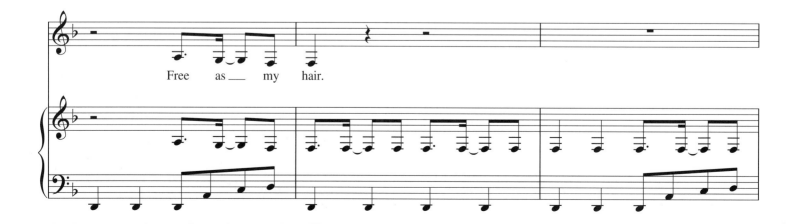

Free as ___ my hair.

I've got my bangs to hide

D.S. al Coda

that I don't stand a chance, a chance.

CODA

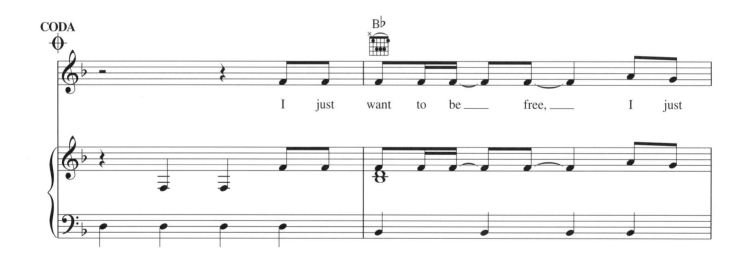

I just want to be free, I just

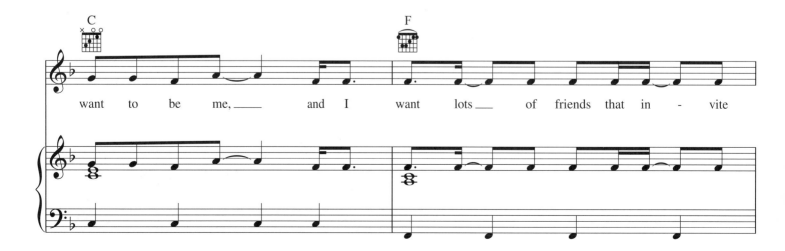

want to be me, and I want lots of friends that in-vite

me to their _ par - ties. I don't want to ___ change _ and I don't

want to be a - shamed. _ I'm the spir - it of my hair, ___ it's all the

glo - ry that I ___ bear. I'm my hair, I'm my hair, _ I'm my hair, I'm my hair, _ I'm my

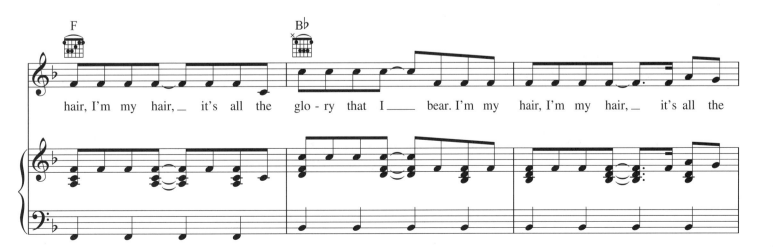

hair, I'm my hair, _ it's all the glo - ry that I ___ bear. I'm my hair, I'm my hair, _ it's all the

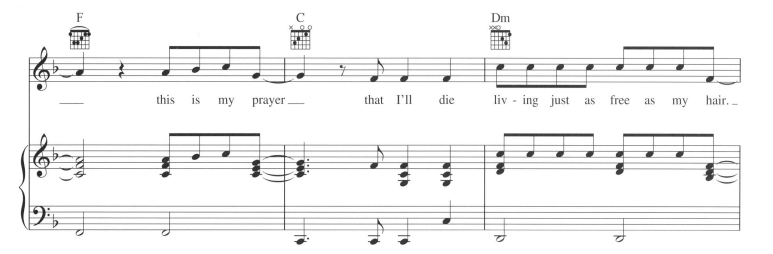

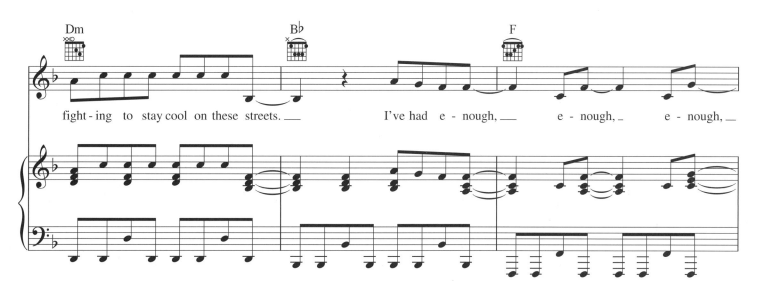

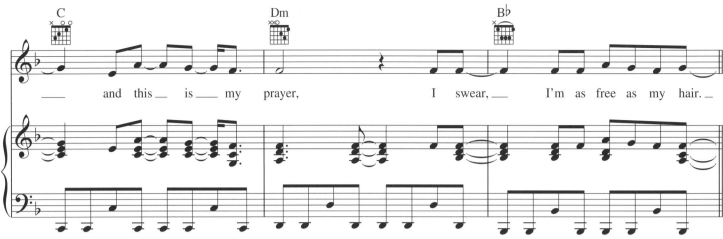

and this ___ is ___ my prayer,   I swear, ___ I'm as free as my hair. ___

___   I'm as free as my hair. ___

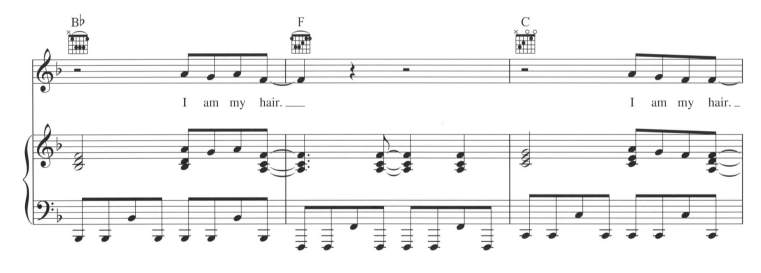

I am my hair. ___   I am my hair. _

Repeat ad lib. and Fade

Optional Ending

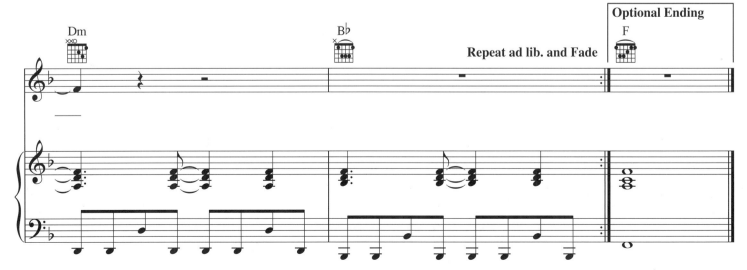

SCHEIßE

Words and Music by STEFANI GERMANOTTA
and NADIR KHAYAT

Dance Pop

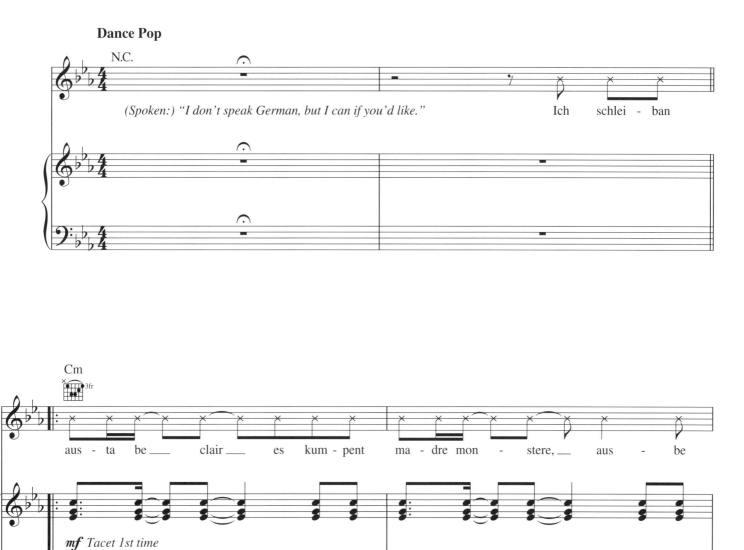

(Spoken:) "I don't speak German, but I can if you'd like."

Ich schlei - ban aus - ta be ___ clair ___ es kum - pent ma - dre mon - stere, ___ aus - be

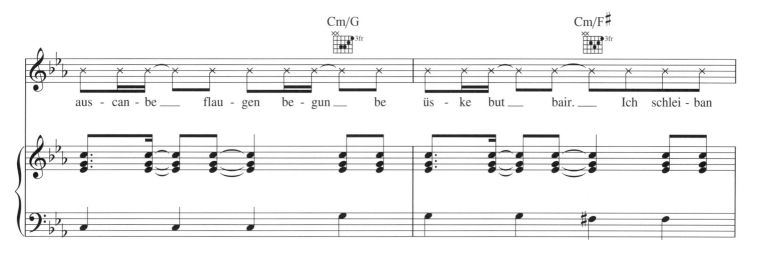

aus - can - be ___ flau - gen be - gun be ü - ske but ___ bair. ___ Ich schlei - ban

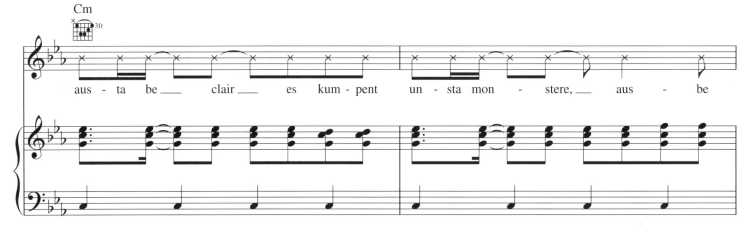

aus - ta be __ clair __ es kum - pent un - sta mon - stere, __ aus - be

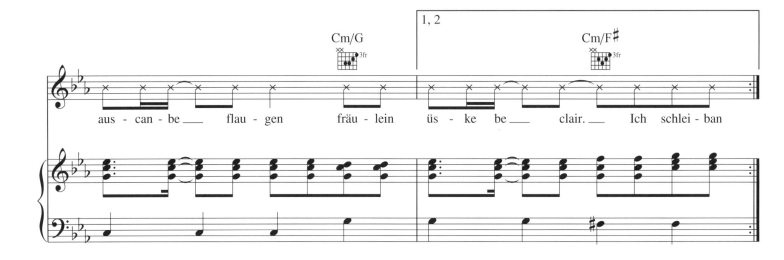

aus - can - be __ flau - gen fräu - lein üs - ke be __ clair. __ Ich schlei - ban

üs - ke be __ clair. __ I'll take you out to - night, __ say what - ev -
jec - ti - fied __ by what men

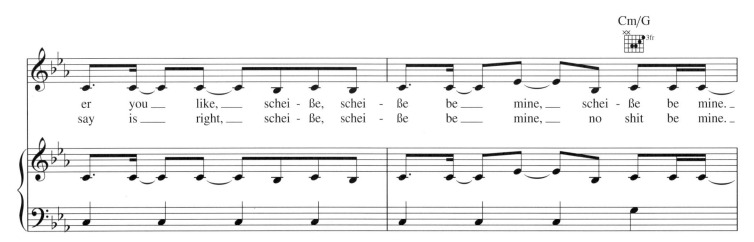

er you __ like, __ schei - ße, schei - ße be __ mine, __ schei - ße be __ mine.
say is __ right, __ schei - ße, schei - ße be __ mine, __ no shit be __ mine.

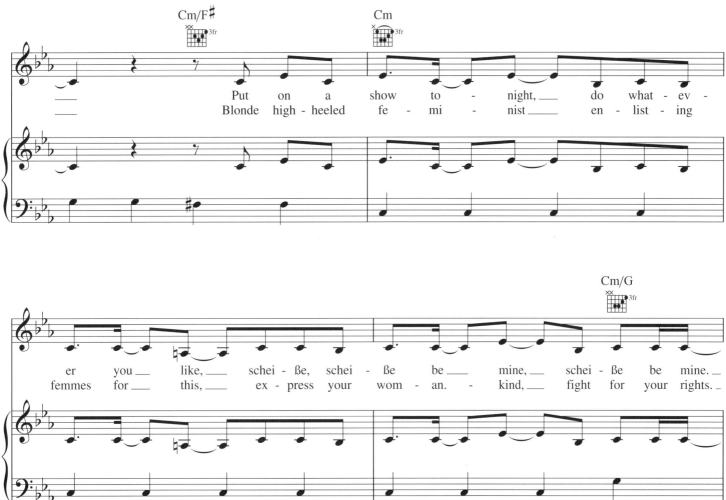

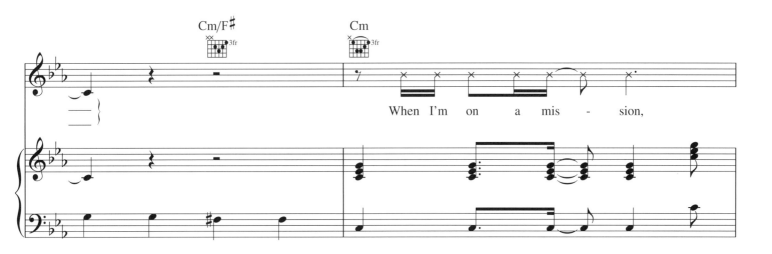

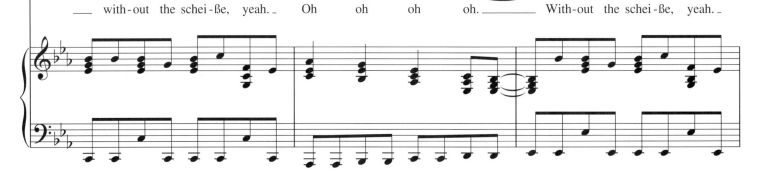

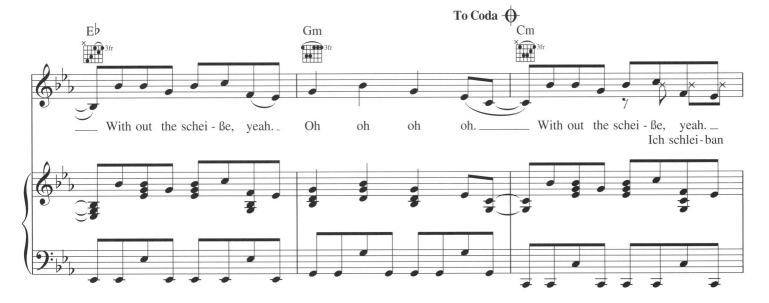

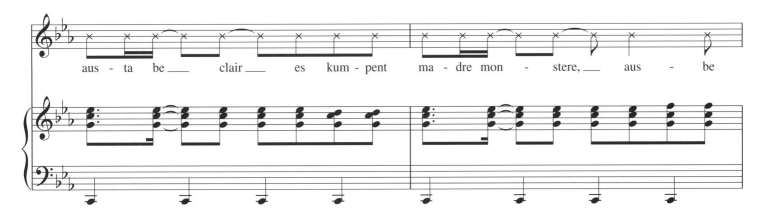

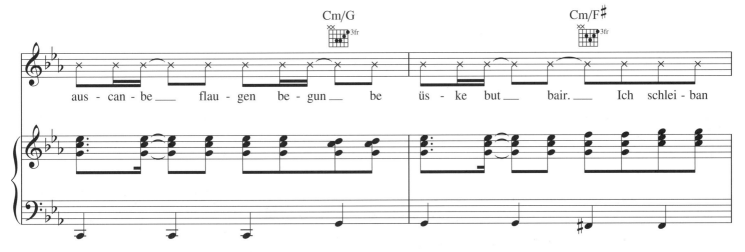

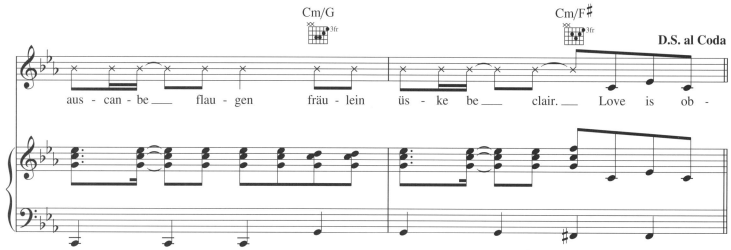

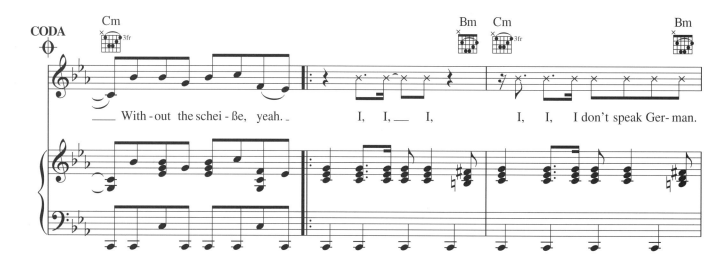

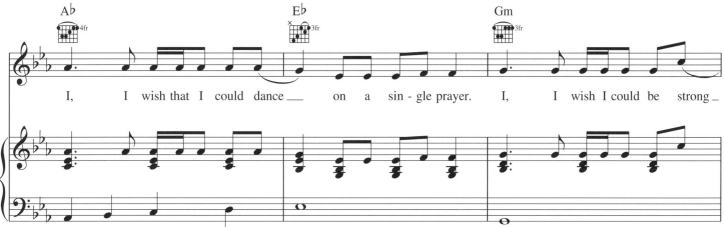

BLOODY MARY

Words and Music by STEFANI GERMANOTTA,
PAUL BLAIR, CLINTON SPARKS, FERNANDO GARIBAY
and WILLIAM GRIGAHCINE

Moderate Pop feel

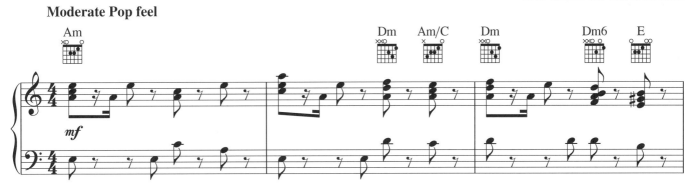

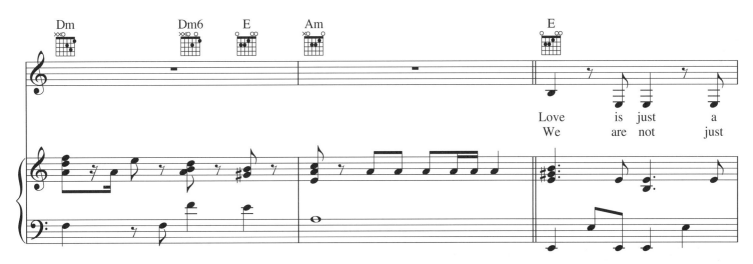

Love is just a just
We are not a just

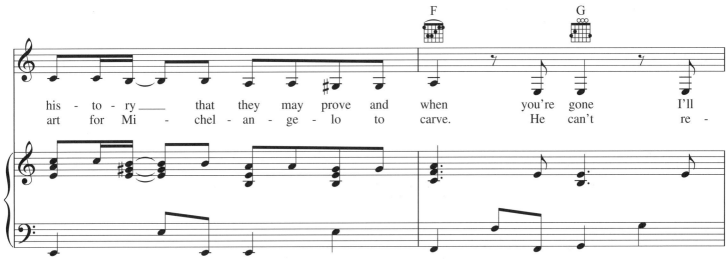

his-to-ry ___ that they may prove and when you're gone I'll
art for Mi-chel-an-ge-lo to carve. He can't re-

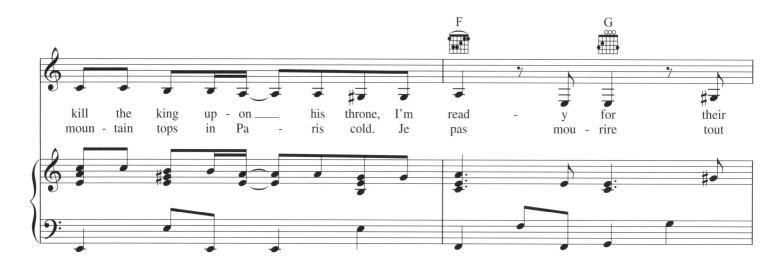

hands, hands, hands a-bove my head._ Hands to-geth-er, for-give him be-fore he's dead be-cause...

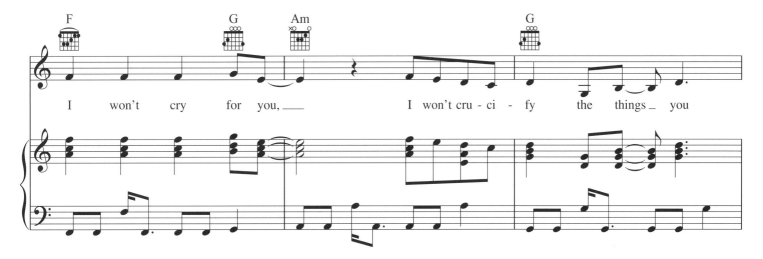

I won't cry for you, ___ I won't cru-ci-fy the things _ you

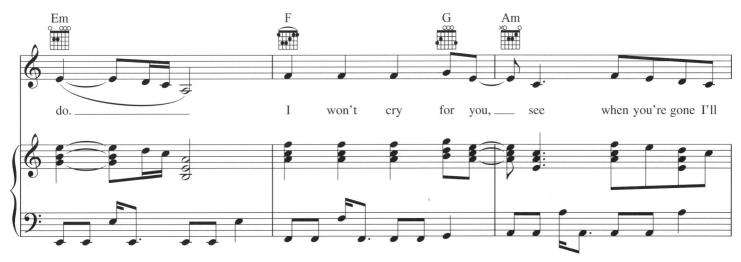

do. _____ I won't cry for you, __ see when you're gone I'll

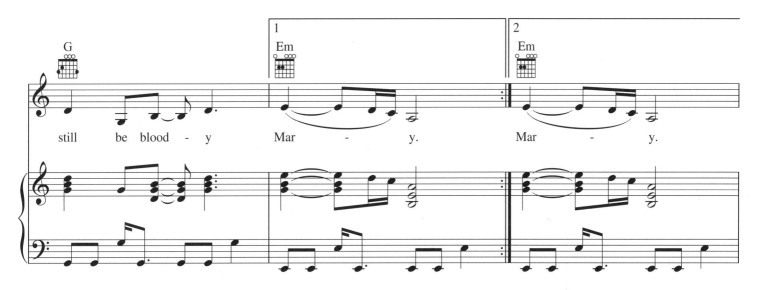

still be blood-y Mar - y. Mar - y.

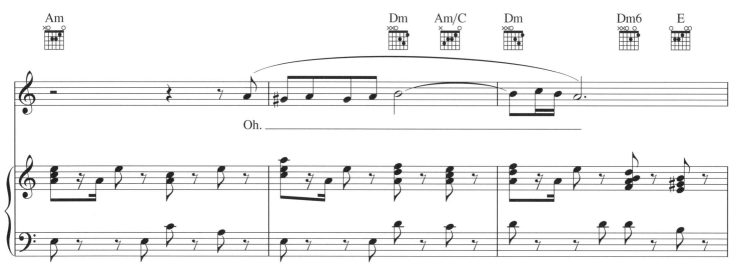

Oh. _____

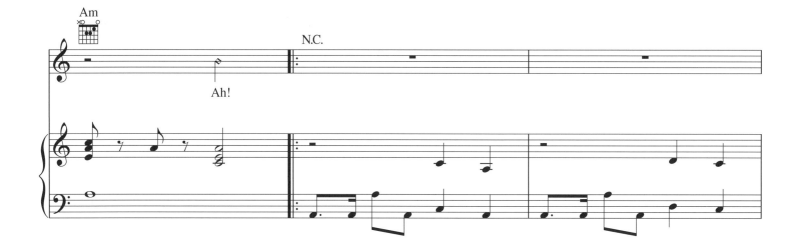

Ah!

Dum dum da di da, ___

dum dum da di da ___ di-di da di da. _____ Dum dum da di da. ___

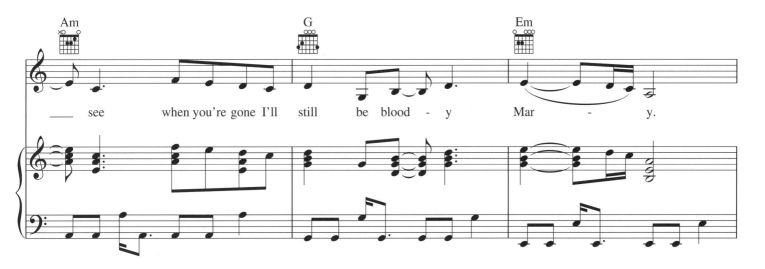

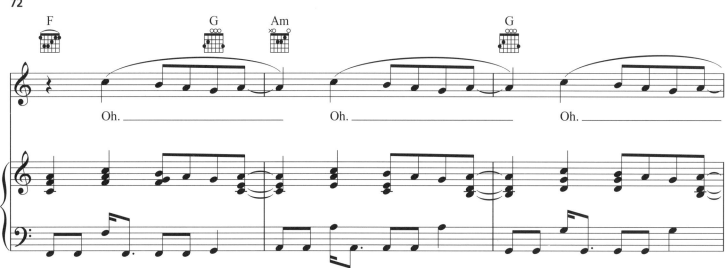

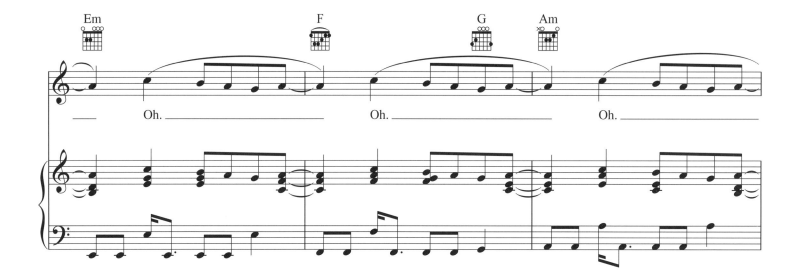

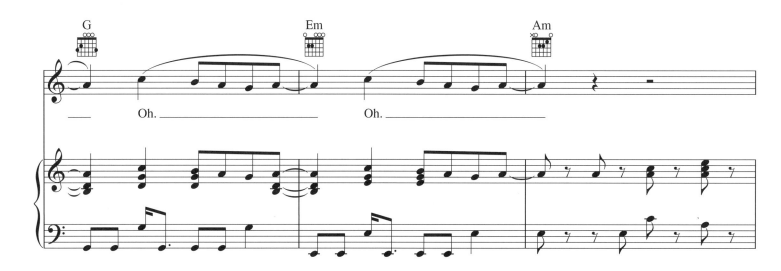

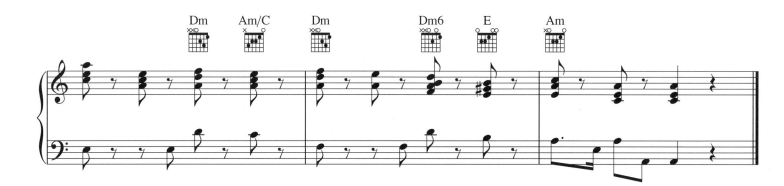

BAD KIDS

Words and Music by STEFANI GERMANOTTA,
JEPPE LAURSEN and PUAL BLAIR

Dance Pop

(Spoken:) *"We don't care what people say, we know the truth."*

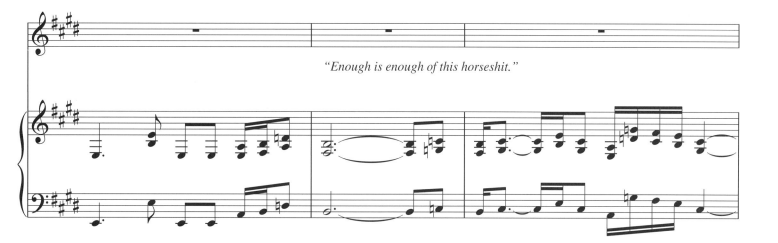

"Enough is enough of this horseshit."

"I am not a freak, I was born with my free gun."   *"Don't tell me I'm less than my freedom."*

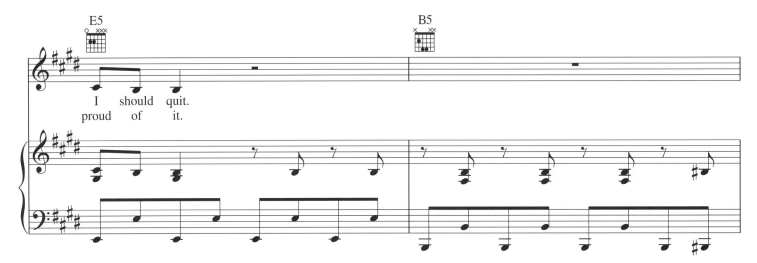

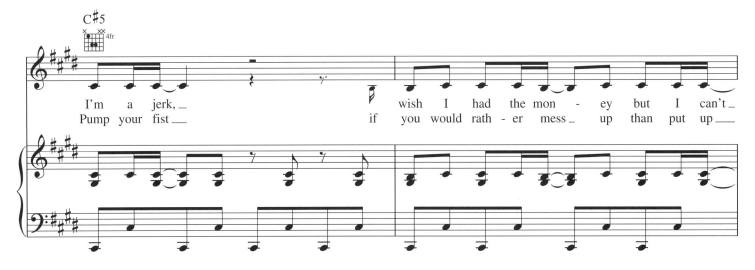

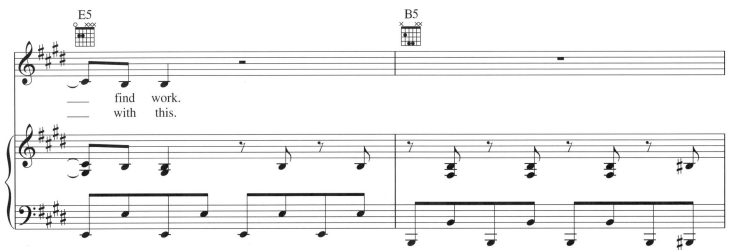

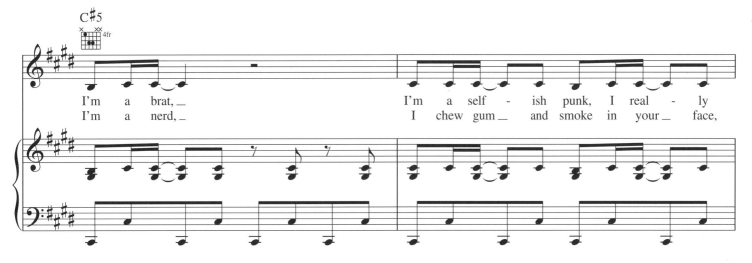

I'm a brat, __ I'm a self - ish punk, I real - ly
I'm a nerd, __ I chew gum __ and smoke in your __ face,

should be smacked.
I'm ab - surd.
My

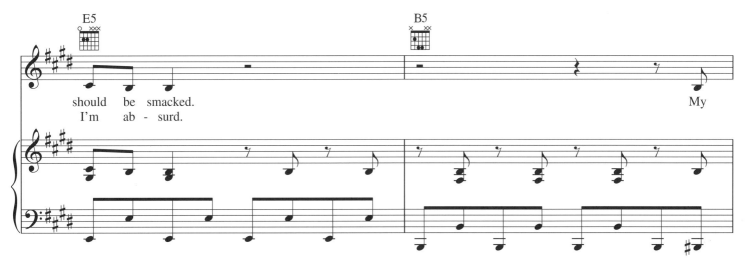

par - ents tried but 'til they got di - vorced __ 'cause I __ ru -
I'm so bad, but I don't give a damn, __ I love __ it __

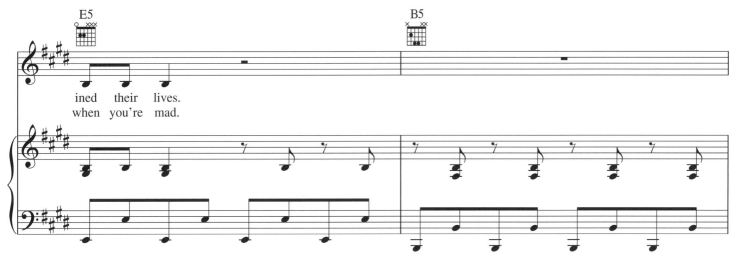

ined their lives.
when you're mad.

I'm a bad ___ kid and I will sur-vive, ___ oh, I'm a

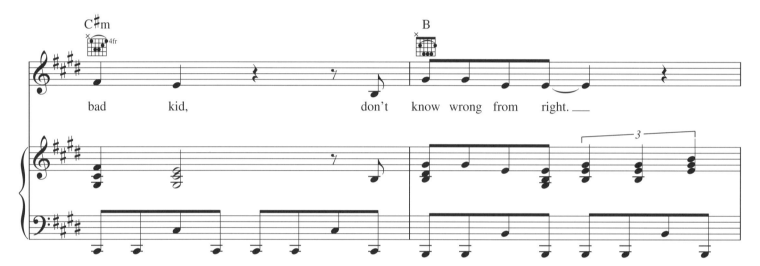

bad kid, don't know wrong from right. ___

I'm a bad ___ kid and this is my life, ___ one of the

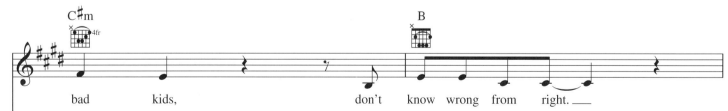

bad kids, don't know wrong from right. ___

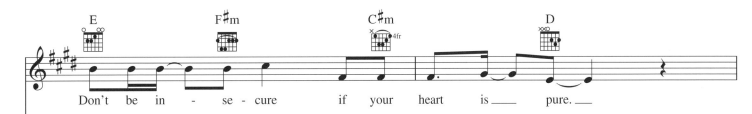

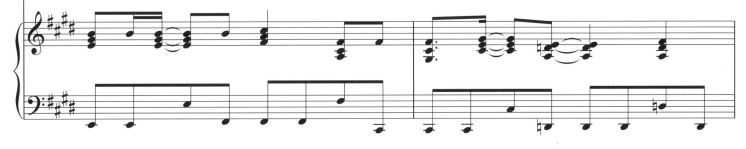

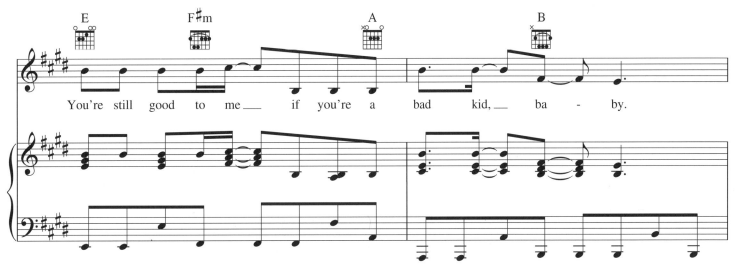

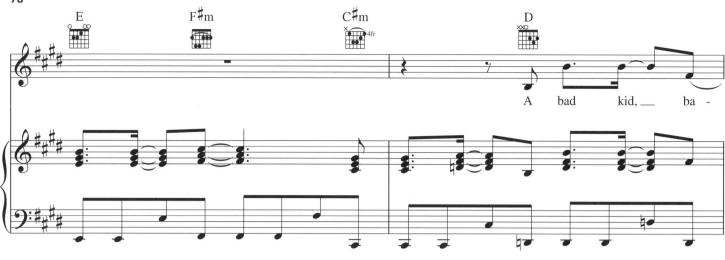

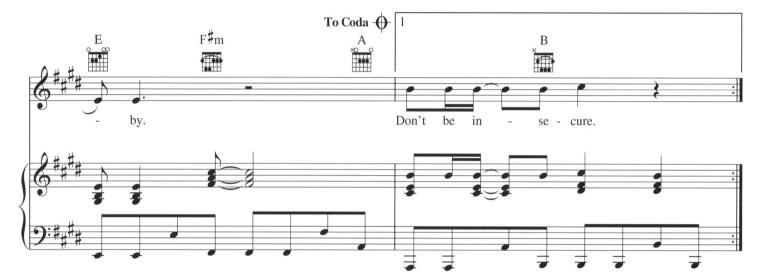

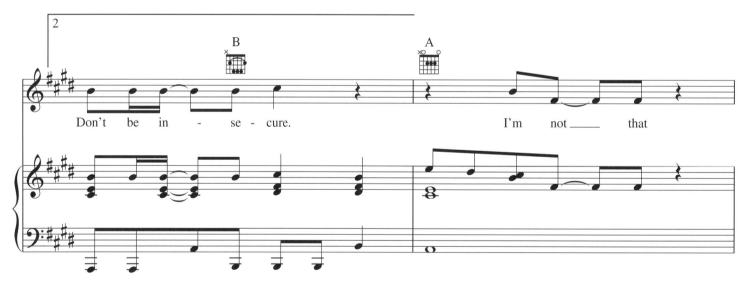

Mom and Dad made __ me. I'm not __ that cool and you hate __ me, I'm a

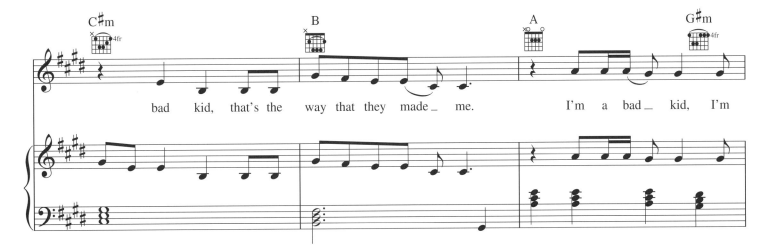

bad kid, that's the way that they made __ me. I'm a bad __ kid, I'm

dis - as - ter - ous, __ give me your mon - ey or I'll hold my breath. __

I'm a bad __ kid and I will sur - vive, __ one of the bad kids, don't

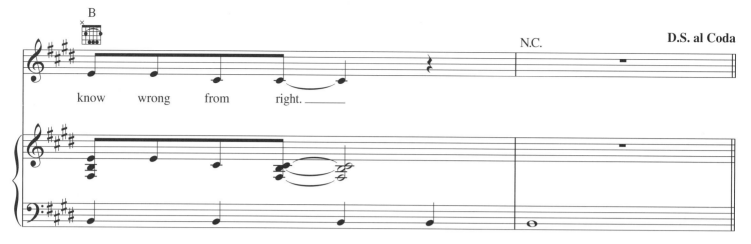

know wrong from right. _____

D.S. al Coda

A bad kid, __ ba - by.

A bad kid, __ ba - by.

A bad kid, __ ba - by.

HIGHWAY UNICORN
(Road to Love)

Words and Music by STEFANI GERMANOTTA,
PAUL BLAIR, FERNANDO GARIBAY
and BRIAN LEE

Electro Pop

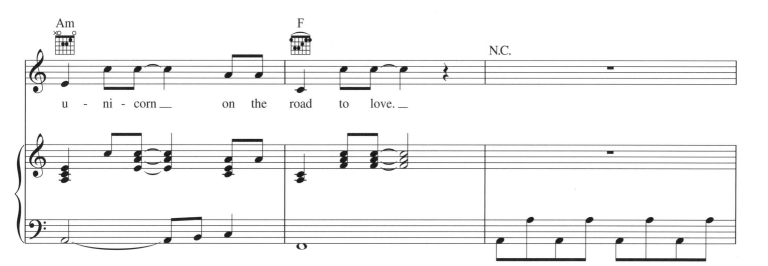

Run,   run   with her...   Run,   run   with her...   Run,   run   with   her...

Run,   run   with her...   Run, run   with her   top   down, ba - by, she   flies.___

F   G

Run,   run   with the

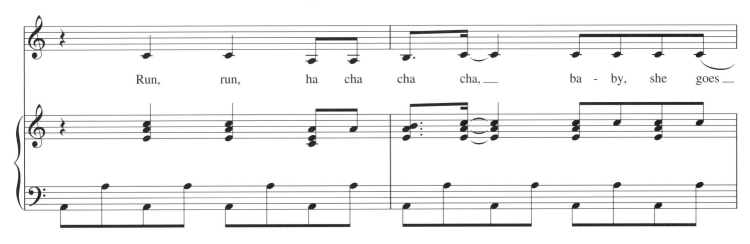

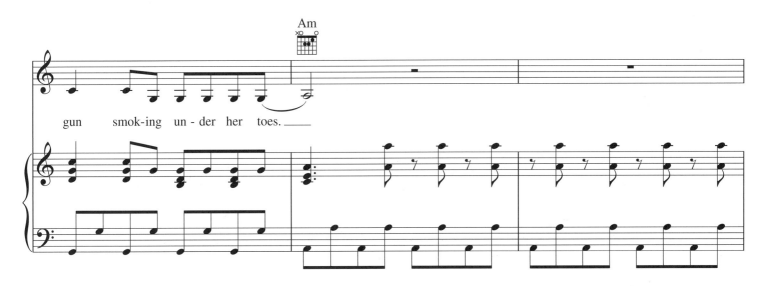

Oh, _____ oh. _____ Ride, ride, po - ny, ride,

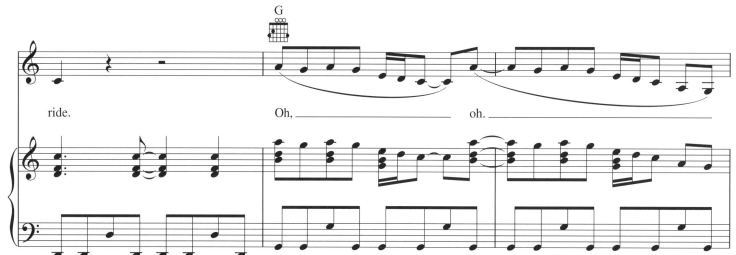

ride. Oh, _____ oh. _____

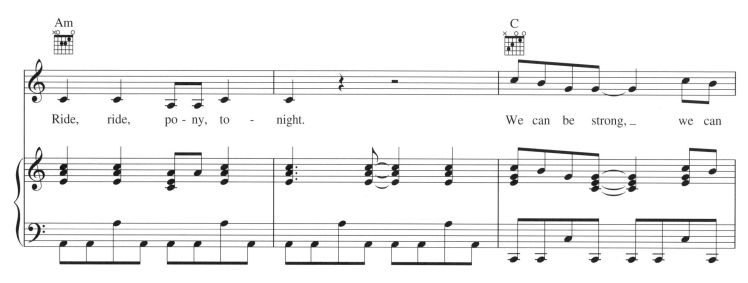

Ride, ride, po - ny, to - night. We can be strong, _ we can

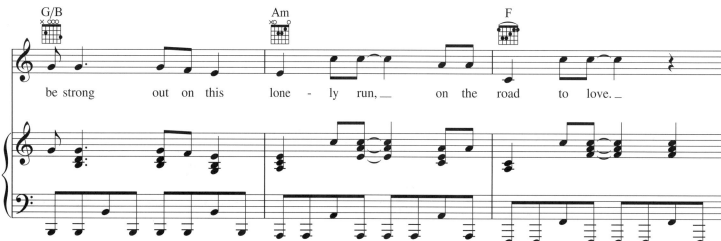

be strong out on this lone - ly run, _ on the road to love. _

We can be strong, __ we can be strong, fol-low that u – ni-corn __ on the

road to love. __ I'm on the road, _____

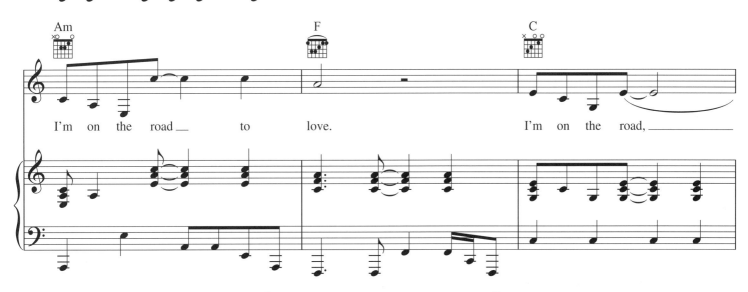

I'm on the road __ to love. I'm on the road, _____

To Coda ⊕

_____ I'm on the road __ to love. _____

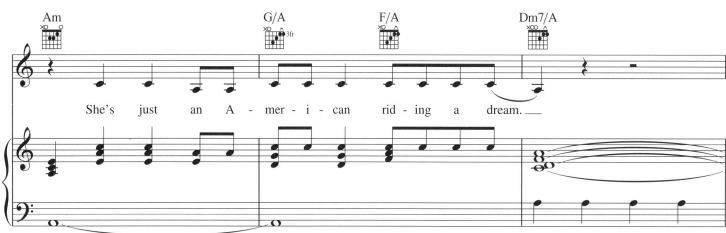

She's just an A-mer-i-can rid-ing a dream. __

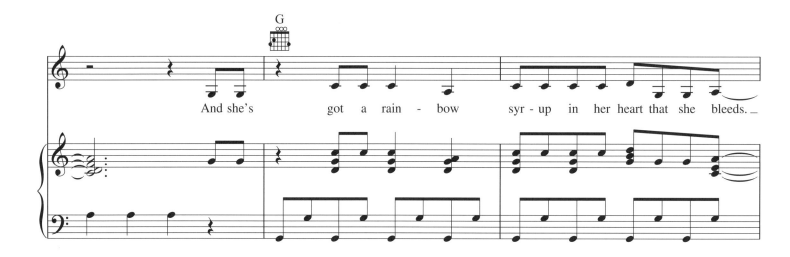

And she's got a rain-bow syr-up in her heart that she bleeds. __

She don't care if your

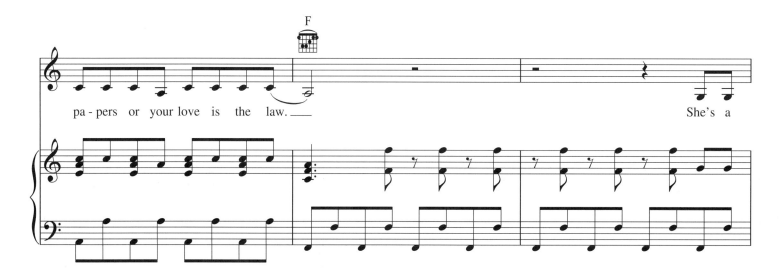

pa-pers or your love is the law. __ She's a

D.S. al Coda

free soul burn-ing roads with a flag in her bra.___

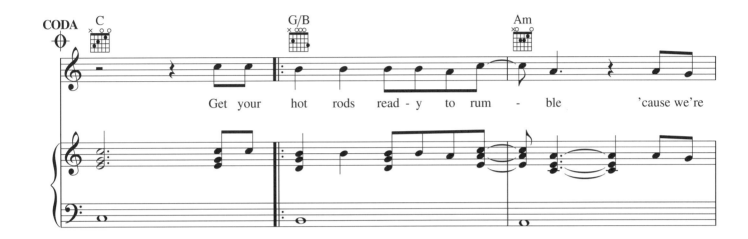

CODA

Get your hot rods read-y to rum-ble 'cause we're

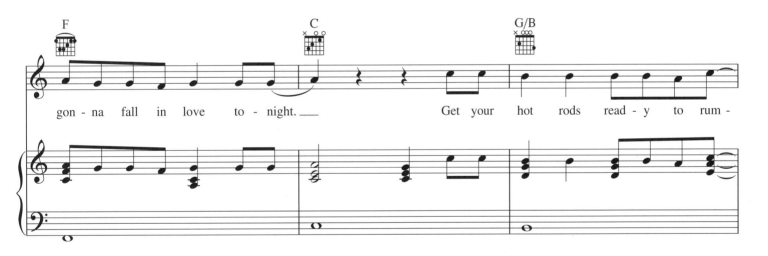

gon-na fall in love to-night.___ Get your hot rods read-y to rum-

-ble 'cause we're gon-na drink un-til we die.___ Get your

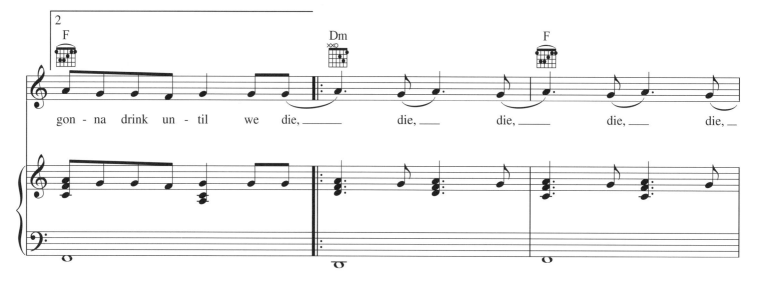

gon - na drink un - til we die, _____ die, ___ die, _____ die, ___ die, _

___ die, ___ die, _____ die, _ die, _____ die, _ die, _____ die, _ die, _

Vocal fade out on repeat

___ die, _ die, _____ die, _ die, _

HEAVY METAL LOVER

Words and Music by STEFANI GERMANOTTA
and FERNANDO GARIBAY

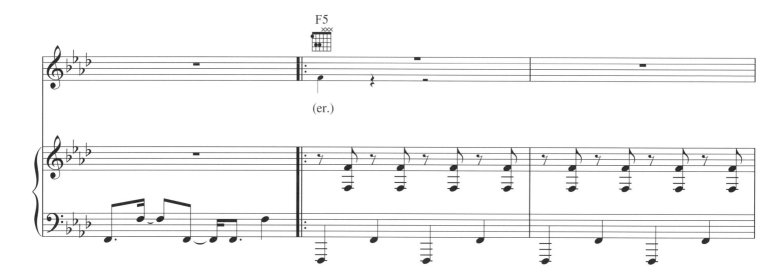

(er.)

1 **2**

Heav - y met - al lov - er. Heav - y met - al lov - er. Heav - y met - al lov -

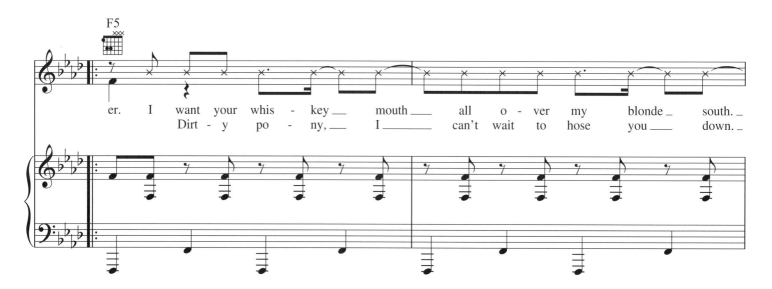

er. I want your whis - key __ mouth __ all o - ver my blonde __ south. __

Dirt - y po - ny, __ I _____ can't wait to hose you __ down. __

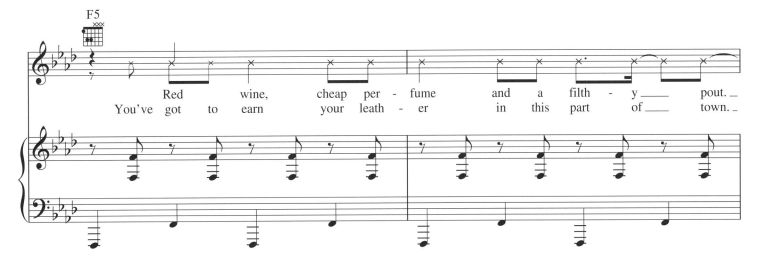

Red wine, cheap per - fume and a filth - y ___ pout. ___
You've got to earn your leath - er in this part of ___ town. ___

To - night bring all your friends ___ be - cause a group does it bet -
Dirt - y pearls and a patch ___ for all the Riv - ing - ton Reb -

ter.
els.

Why riv - er with a pair, ___ let's have a house full of leath -
Let's raise hell in the streets, ___ drink beer and get in - to trou -

er. }
ble. }

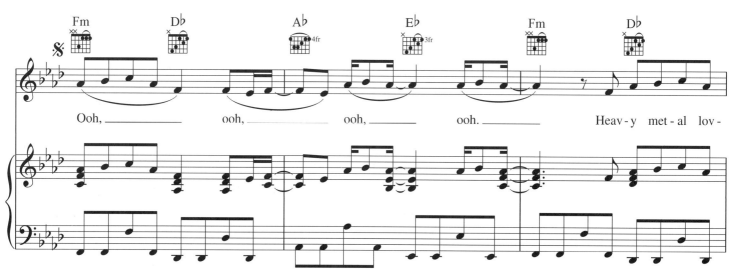

Ooh, _____ ooh, _____ ooh, _____ ooh. _____ Heav-y met-al lov-

er.　　　　Ooh, _____ ooh, _____ ooh, _____ ooh. _____

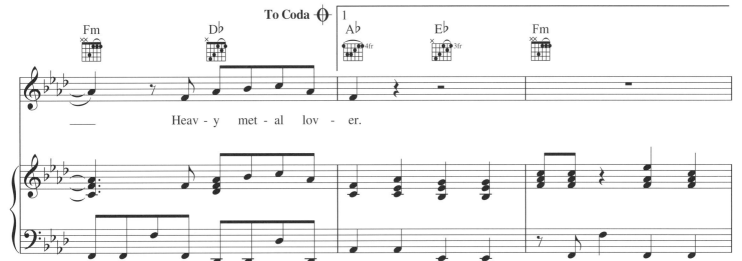

To Coda ⊕

Heav - y met - al lov - er.

er.　I could be your girl, girl, __ girl, girl, __ girl, __ girl. __ But would you

love me if I ruled the world, world, world? Ooh, ooh,

ooh, ooh. Heav-y met-al lov-er.

Whip me, slap me, punk funk, New York club-bers, dump drunk.

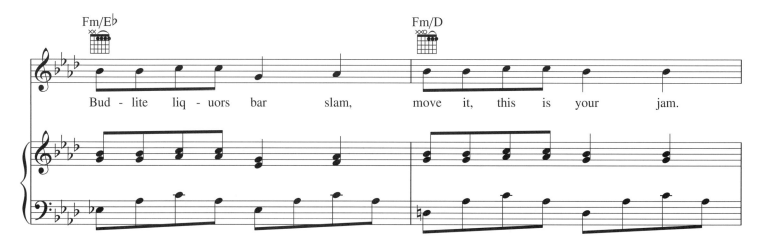

Bud-lite liq-uors bar slam, move it, this is your jam.

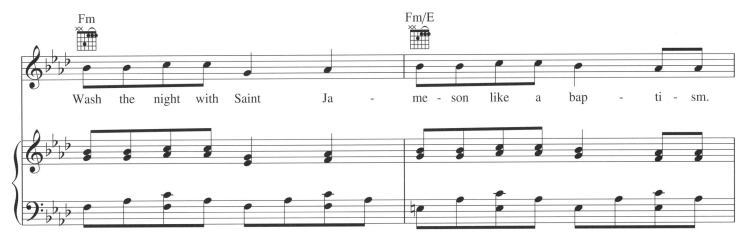

Wash the night with Saint Ja - me - son like a bap - ti - sm.

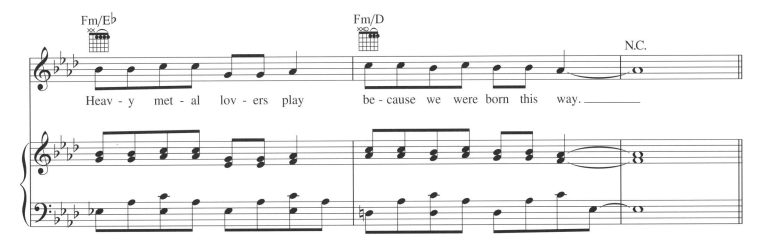

Heav - y met - al lov - ers play be - cause we were born this way. _____

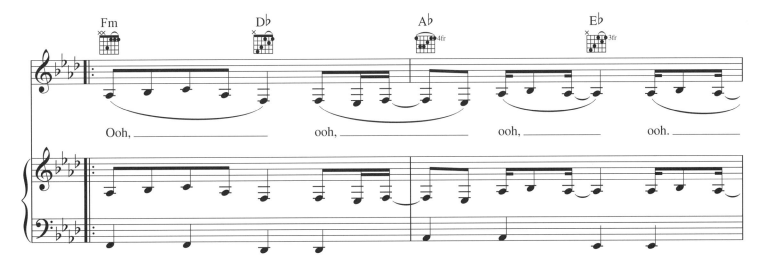

Ooh, _____ ooh, _____ ooh, _____ ooh. _____

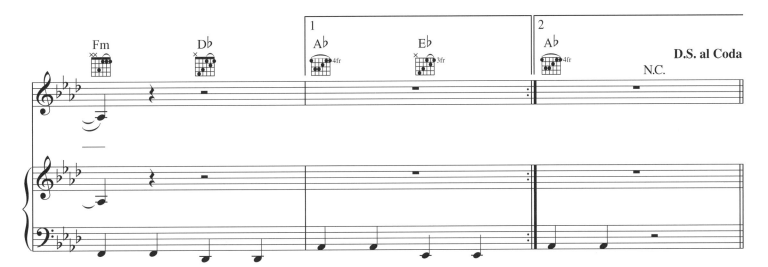

D.S. al Coda

ELECTRIC CHAPEL

Words and Music by STEFANI GERMANOTTA
and PAUL BLAIR

Pop Rock

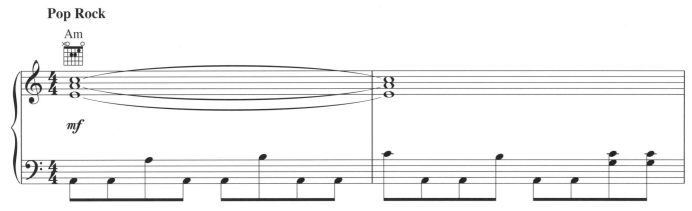

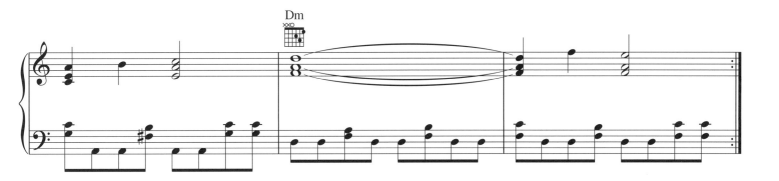

My bod - y is _____ sanc - tu - ar - y, my blood is pure. ___
Con - fess to me _____ where you have been, next to the bar. ___

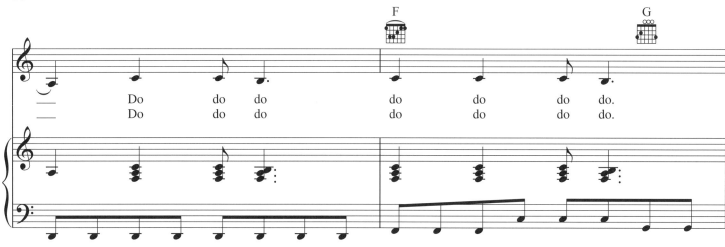

You want me bad, ____ I think you're cool, ____ but I'm not sure. ____

Pray for your sins ____ right un - der the glass dis - co ball. ____

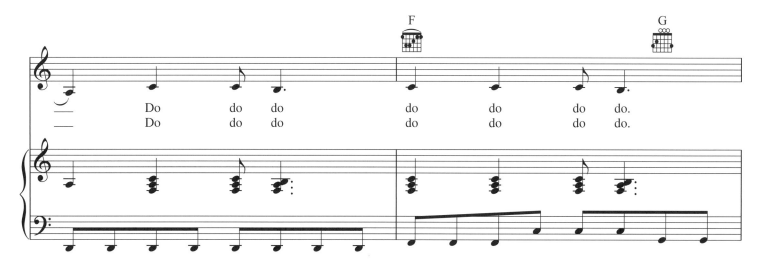

Do do do do do do do.

Do do do do do do do.

Fol - low ____ me, don't ____ be such a ho - ly fool.

Fol - low ____ me, don't ____ be such a ho - ly fool.

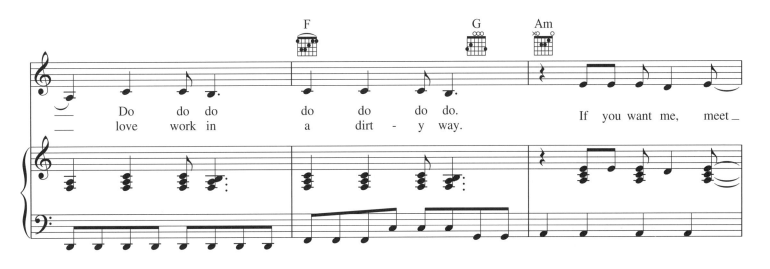

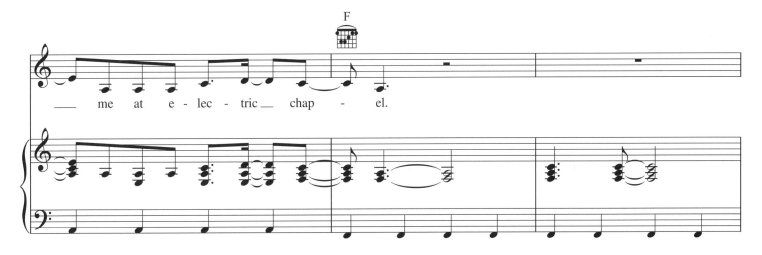

If you want me, meet___ me at e-lec-tric___ chap - el.

If you want to steal my heart a - way,___

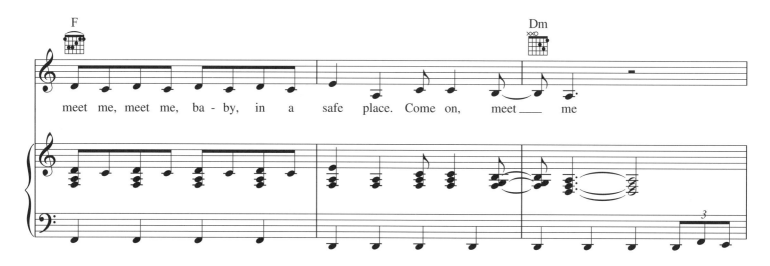

meet me, meet me, ba - by, in a safe place. Come on, meet___ me

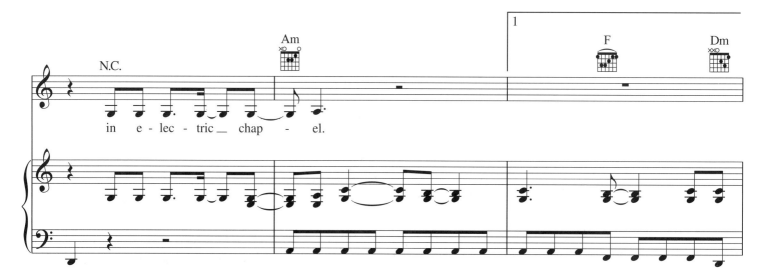

in e-lec-tric___ chap - el.

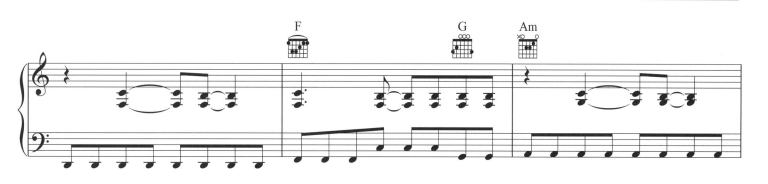

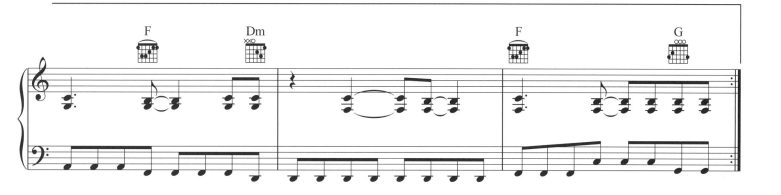

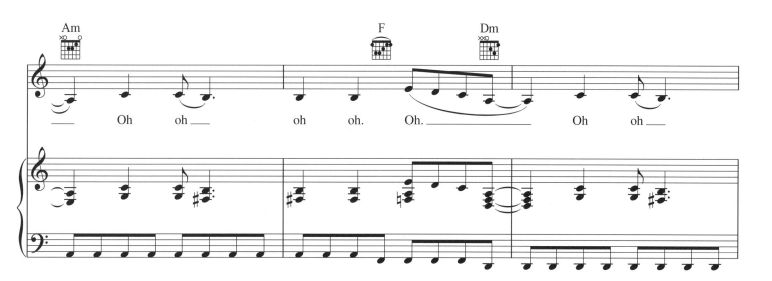

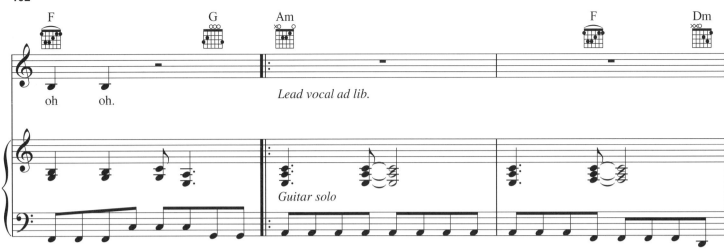

oh oh.

Lead vocal ad lib.

Guitar solo

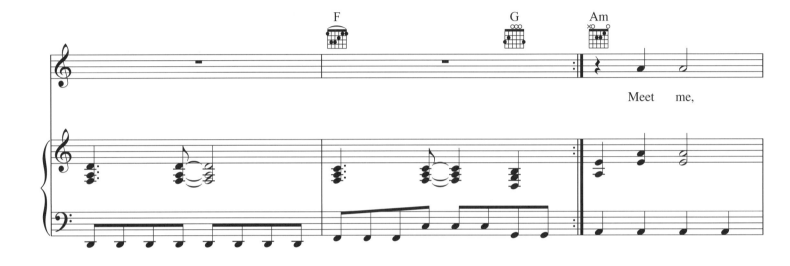

Meet me,

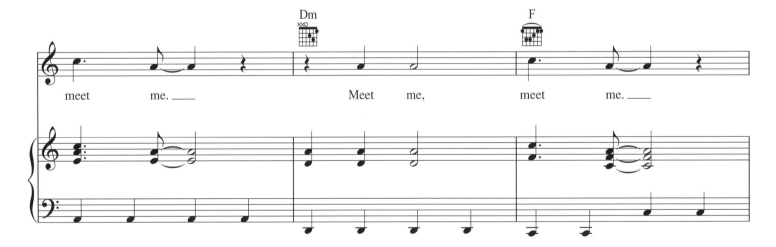

meet me. ___ Meet me, meet me. ___

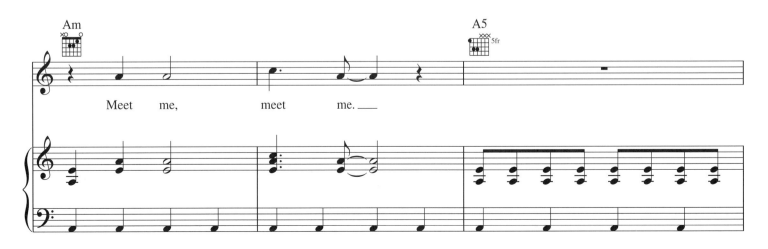

Meet me, meet me. ___

If you want me,__ meet__ me in e-lec-tric__ chap-

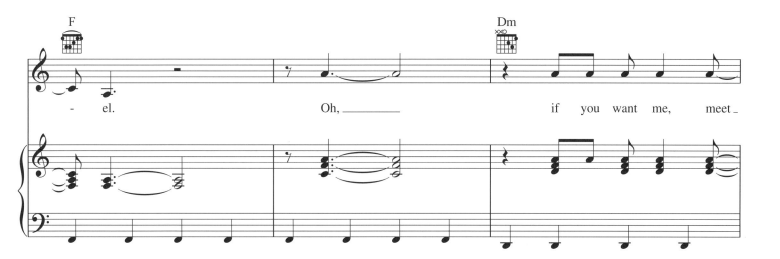

-el. Oh,_____ if you want me, meet__

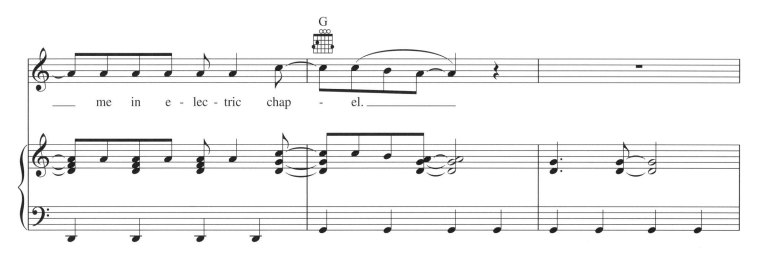

__ me in e-lec-tric chap - el._____

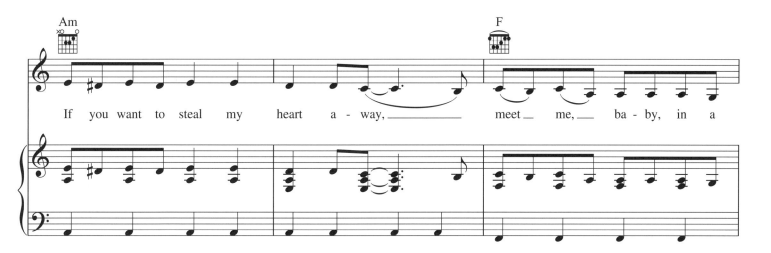

If you want to steal my heart a-way,_____ meet__ me,__ ba-by, in a

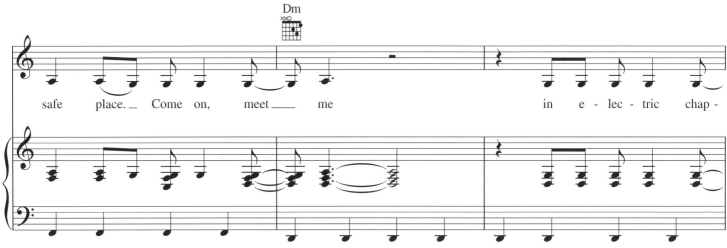

safe place. Come on, meet me in e - lec - tric chap -

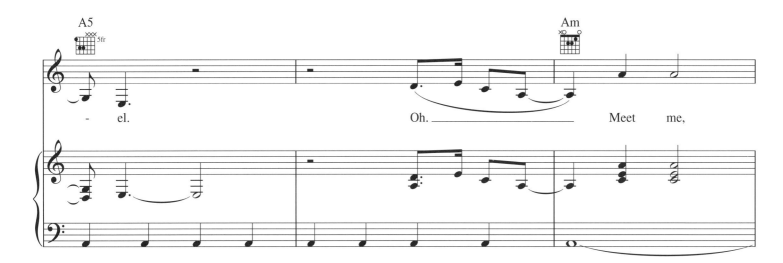

- el. Oh. Meet me,

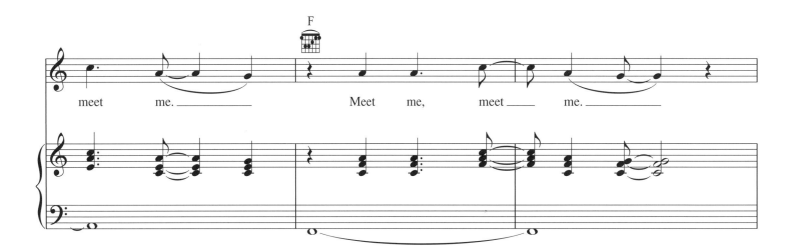

meet me. Meet me, meet me.

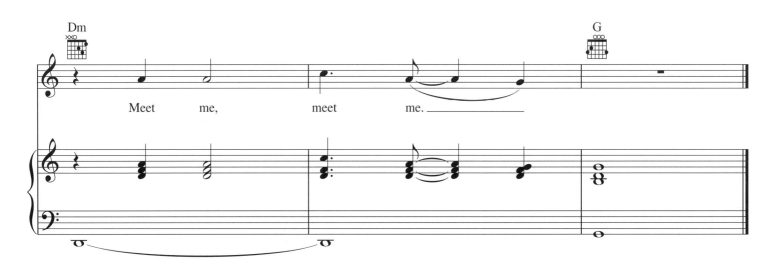

Meet me, meet me.

YOÜ AND I

Words and Music by
STEFANI GERMANOTTA

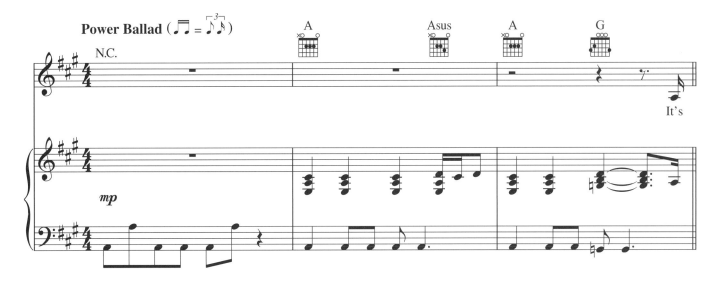

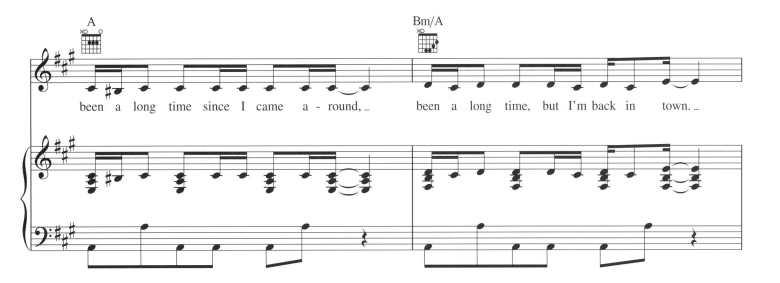

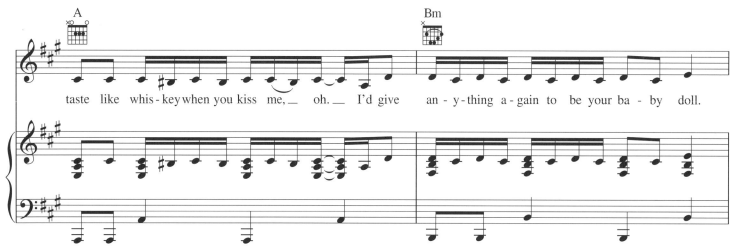

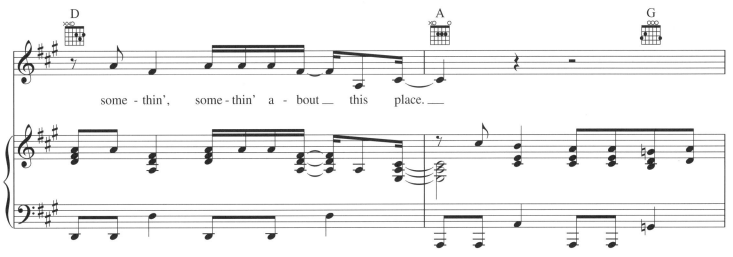

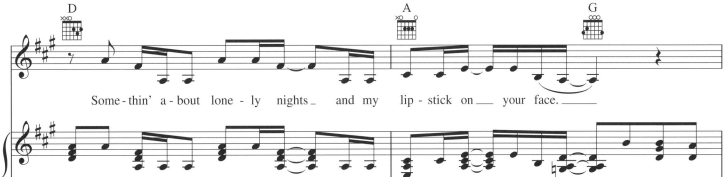

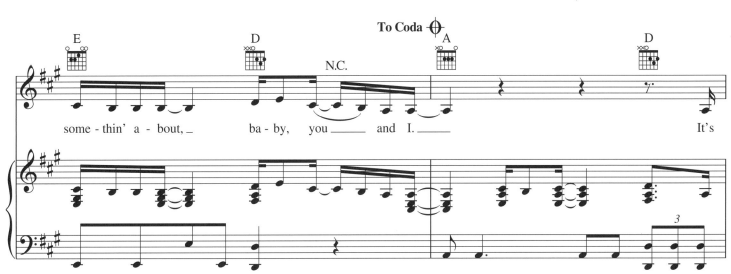

We've got a whole lot o' mon-ey, but we still pay __ rent __ 'cause you

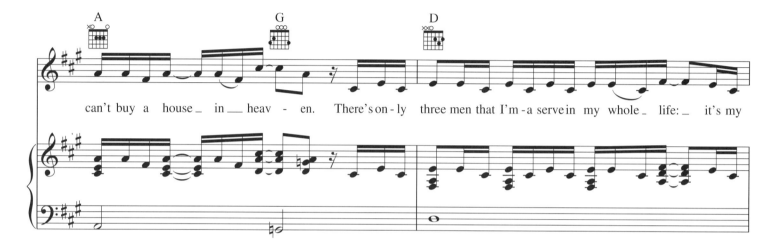

can't buy a house __ in __ heav-en. There's on-ly three men that I'm-a serve in my whole __ life: __ it's my

dad-dy and Ne-bras-ka and __ Je-sus __ Christ. __ There's some-thin', some-thin' a-bout __ the chase. __

__ Six whole years! __ I'm a New York wom-an, born to run you down. So, want my

I. _____ You __ and I. __ I. _____ It's

been a long time _ since I came a - round, _ been a long time, _ but I'm back in town. _ And

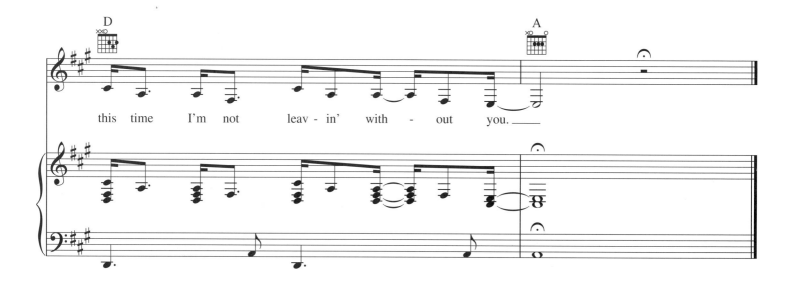

this time I'm not leav - in' with - out you. _____

THE EDGE OF GLORY

Words and Music by STEFANI GERMANOTTA,
PAUL BLAIR and FERNANDO GARIBAY

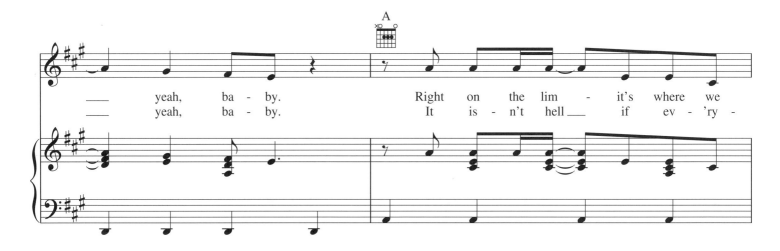

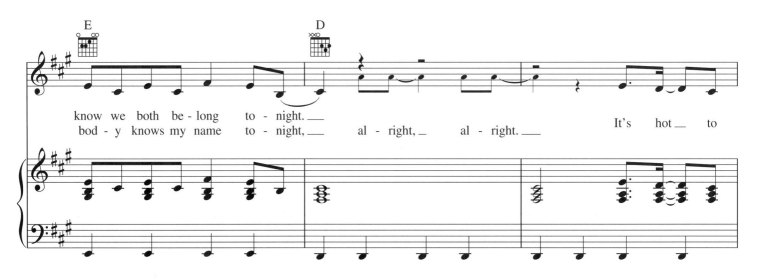

feel the ____ rush, ____ to brush the dan - ger - ous.

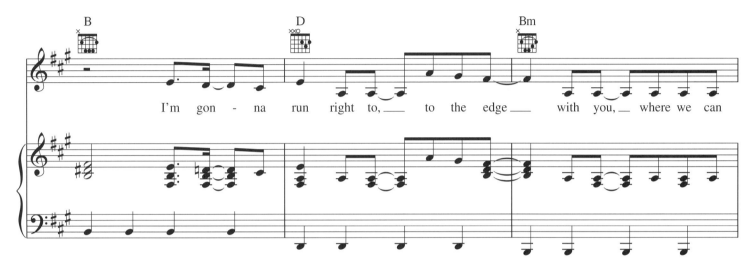

I'm gon - na run right to, ___ to the edge ___ with you, __ where we can

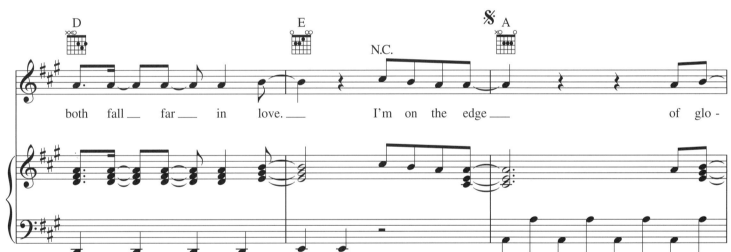

both fall ___ far ___ in love. ___ I'm on the edge ___ of glo -

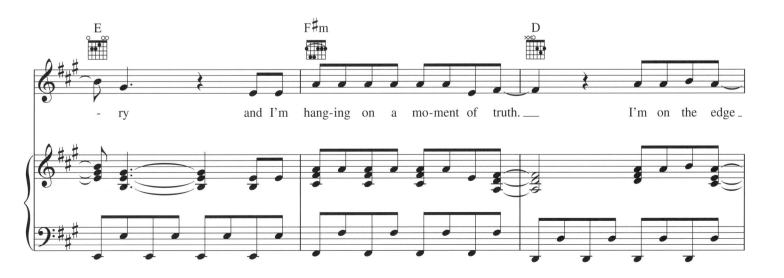

- ry and I'm hang-ing on a mo-ment of truth. ___ I'm on the edge __

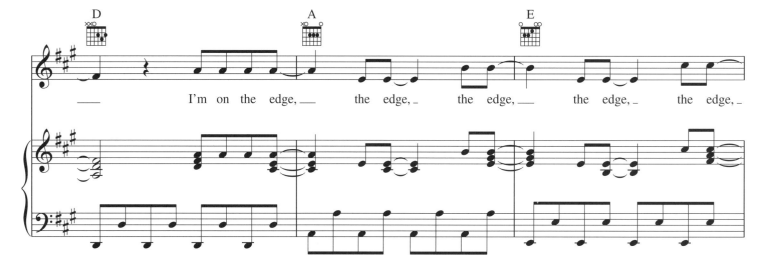

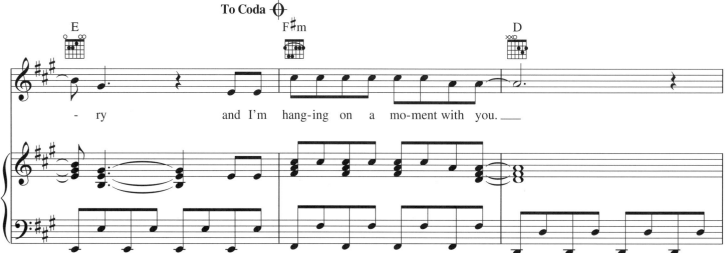

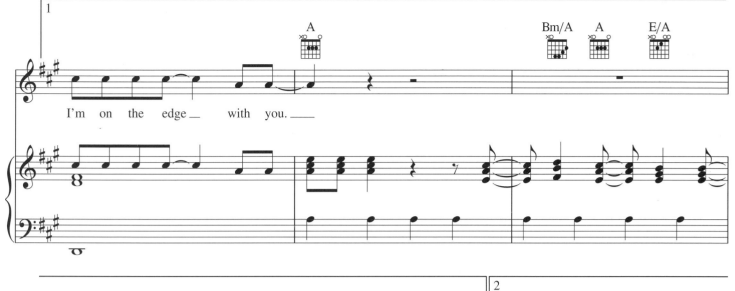

I'm on the edge __ with you. ____

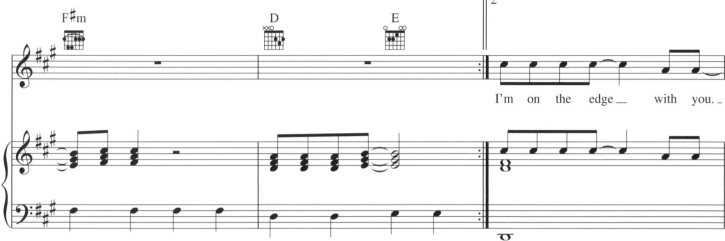

I'm on the edge __ with you. _

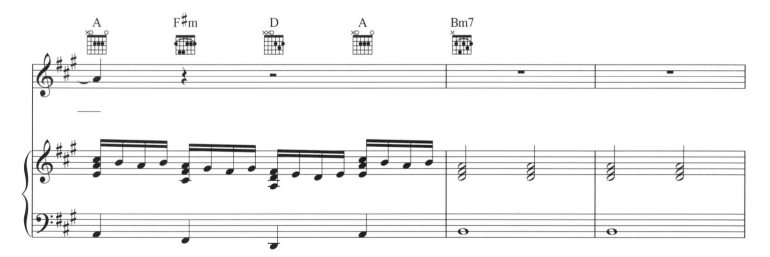

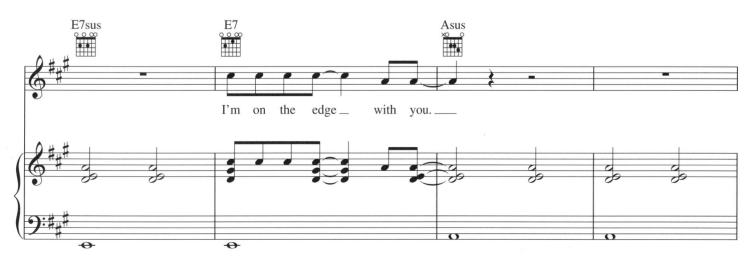

I'm on the edge __ with you. ____

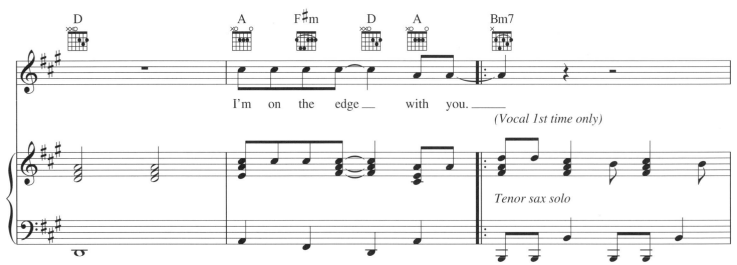

I'm on the edge ___ with you. ____

(Vocal 1st time only)

Tenor sax solo

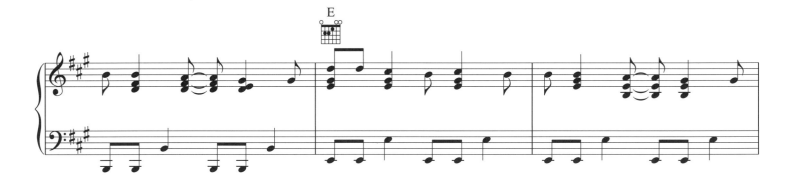

Sax solo ends

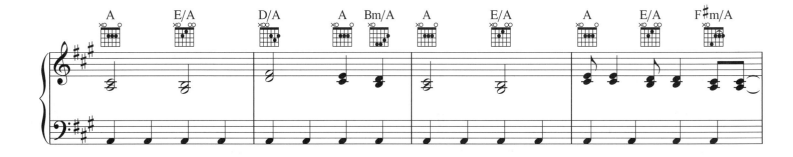

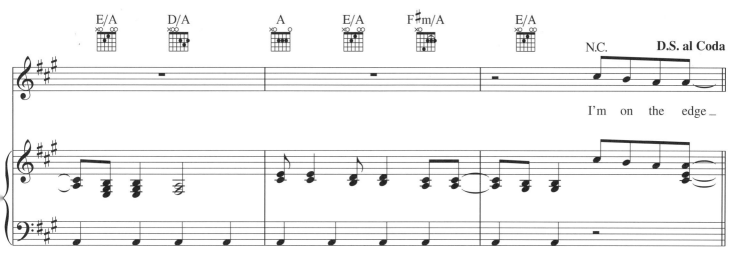